PRINT'S BEST CORPORATE PUBLICATIONS

PRINT'S BEST CORPORATE PUBLICATIONS

Library of Congress Catalog Card
Number 90-091991
ISBN 0–915734–68–0

RC PUBLICATIONS

President and Publisher: Howard Cadel
Vice President and Editor: Martin Fox
Creative Director: Andrew Kner
Managing Director, Book Projects: Linda Silver
Associate Art Director: Thomas Guarnieri

Print's Best
CORPORATE
PUBLICATIONS

WINNING DESIGNS FROM PRINT MAGAZINE'S NATIONAL COMPETITION

Edited by

LINDA SILVER and
TERESA REESE

Art Directed by

ANDREW KNER

Designed by

THOMAS GUARNIERI

Published by

RC PUBLICATIONS, INC.
NEW YORK, NY

INTRODUCTION

Modern image-making as we know it today was born and came of age in the 20th century. Spawned by the advances in printing techniques that began in the late 1800s, the ability to reach and influence millions of people has grown with each new advance in communications. As the technologies of print, film, television, and the computer were being perfected, so was their use in promoting the image of people, places, and things. Side by side with advertising, the most direct method of promotion, has grown a communications industry, called public relations for want of a better name, that uses subtler means than advertising but reaches a more select audience. Included in this category of communications are the corporate publications that enable a company or institution to deliver information and project an image—the desired perception of the company—to carefully targeted groups. These may include a company's employees, present and potential customers, shareholders, and business, financial, media and community leaders.

The examples of corporate publications showcased in this book are divided into five categories: Booklets and Brochures (80 examples), Magazines (12), Catalogs and Manuals (9), Calendars (16), and Special Promotions (23). They were published in recent editions of PRINT's Regional Design Annual, winners of a national competition judged by the editors and art director of PRINT magazine. Here, we are able to devote more space to the selected entries than is possible in the Annual. We may, for example, show spreads from a publication in addition to the previously published cover, or additional covers or spreads from other issues of the publication, or additional promotional items or calendar pages.

The examples collected here represent work of companies ranging from small to some of the biggest corporations in the country and, indeed, in the world. They reflect, in general, a return to more disciplined, tradition-rooted design. This could be tied to the economic downturn of the period in which they were

4

CONTENTS

produced—tight money usually signals a shift to a conservative mood—or a reaction to the graphic excesses of the opulent years of the '80s decade.

Catalogs and manuals keep a company's sales force, as well as wholesale and/or retail customers, informed of the latest models, styles, prices, etc. Graphic merit is especially high in catalogs for paper, textile, and fine home and office furniture companies.

The modern calendar was invented by Pope Gregory XIII in 1582 but did not become commonplace until the reduction in printing costs in the late 19th and early 20th centuries allowed enterprises like insurance companies and banks, or even the local coal and ice company, to distribute free calendars to the public. These early versions have evolved into a $10-billion-a-year calendar business as their users have learned that the calendar, especially when wall-hung, is a year-long, attention-holding medium.

Special promotions range from conservative—booklets or books, albeit embellished with lively graphics or unusual shapes and formats—to extravagant boxes and die-cut productions.

Booklets and brochures can tell the story of a company or a particular corporate endeavor, a real estate development, perhaps, or the introduction of a new product, in much more detail than an ad and without the barrage of statistics in the annual report.

The annual report, in fact, works along with other company publications, especially the magazine that reaches a large audience within and outside a company. Not limited to once a year, the magazine can report a company's accomplishments and project its viewpoints every month or two. Some of these publications rival consumer magazines in their graphic layouts and editorial content and, as demonstrated in this book, in their printing and production values. —*Teresa Reese*

1.

Cover (1), spreads (2,3) and spot illustration (4) from promotional brochure on "De Stijl"— part of a series on historical graphic styles. DESIGN FIRM: The Pushpin Group, New York, New York

ART DIRECTOR/ DESIGNER/ ILLUSTRATOR: Seymour Chwast

ASSOCIATE DESIGNER: Roxanne Slimak

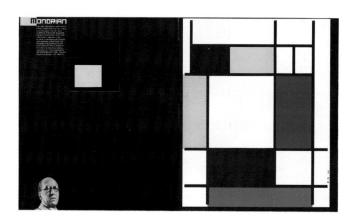

2.

3.

Mohawk Paper

Paper products

4.

6

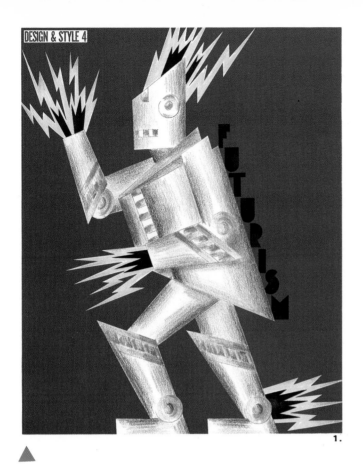

DESIGN & STYLE 4

1.

WAAAAAAAA

GHHROO

"A Racing Car WHOSE HEAD IS ADORNED WITH GREAT PIPES.... IS MORE BEAUTIFUL THAN THE Victory OF Samothrace."

VRUUUUUUUM

3.

DINAMO
DEPERO
FUTURISTA

DINAMO

DINAMO-AZARI
DEPERO
FVTVRISTA

4.

2.

Cover (1), spreads (3,4) and spot illustration (2) from promotional brochure on "Italian Futurism & Art Deco"— part of a series on historical graphic styles. **DESIGN FIRM:** The Pushpin Group, New York, New York

ART DIRECTOR/ DESIGNER/ ILLUSTRATOR: Seymour Chwast **ASSOCIATE DESIGNER:** Roxanne Slimak

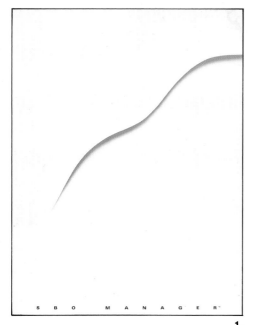

1.

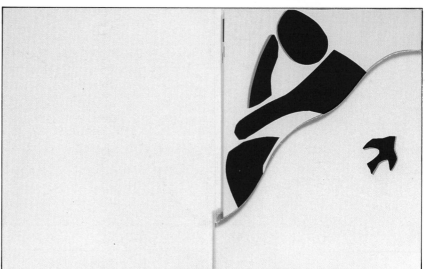

2.

FIRST, DO NO HARM.

3.

EVOLUTION.

4.

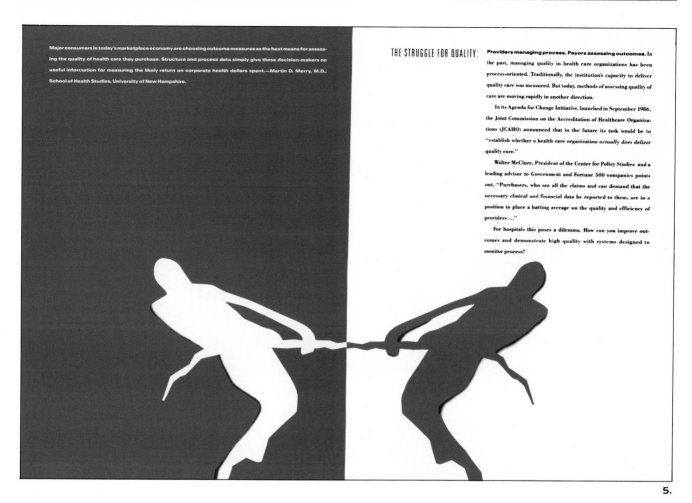

Major consumers in today's marketplace economy are choosing outcome measures as the best means for assessing the quality of health care they purchase. Structure and process data simply give these decision-makers no useful information for measuring the likely return on corporate health dollars spent.—Martin D. Merry, M.D., School of Health Studies, University of New Hampshire.

THE STRUGGLE FOR QUALITY:

Providers managing process. Payors assessing outcomes. In the past, managing quality in health care organizations has been process-oriented. Traditionally, the institution's *capacity* to deliver quality care was measured. But today, methods of assessing quality of care are moving rapidly in another direction.

In its Agenda for Change Initiative, launched in September 1986, the Joint Commission on the Accreditation of Healthcare Organizations (JCAHO) announced that in the future its task would be to "establish whether a health care organization *actually does deliver* quality care."

Walter McClure, President of the Center for Policy Studies and a leading advisor to Government and Fortune 500 companies points out, "Purchasers, who see all the claims and can demand that the necessary clinical and financial data be reported to them, are in a position to place a batting average on the quality and efficiency of providers…"

For hospitals this poses a dilemma. How can you improve outcomes and demonstrate high quality with systems designed to monitor process?

5.

Cover (1) and interior (2) of pocket folder containing series of promotional brochures explaining software system; covers (3,4), spread (5) and detail (6) from brochures.
DESIGN FIRM: The Design Office of Hedi Yamada and More Often than Not, Jill Stone, Irvine, California
DESIGNER: Jill Stone
DESIGNER/ILLUSTRATOR: Hedi Yamada
ILLUSTRATOR: Mark Sasway

6.

HCA HOUSTON INTERNATIONAL HOSPITAL

1.

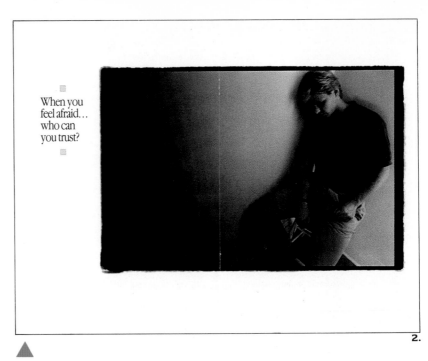

When you
feel afraid…
who can
you trust?

2.

HCA Houston International Hospital

Health care

Cover (1) and spread (2) from general capabilities brochure for a psychiatric facility; covers (3) of brochure inserts that focus on specific areas of concern.

DESIGN FIRM: Artisan Field Design, Houston, Texas

DESIGNERS: Mary Boyles, Tom Boyles

PHOTOGRAPHER: Greg Dawson

ILLUSTRATOR: Mary Boyles

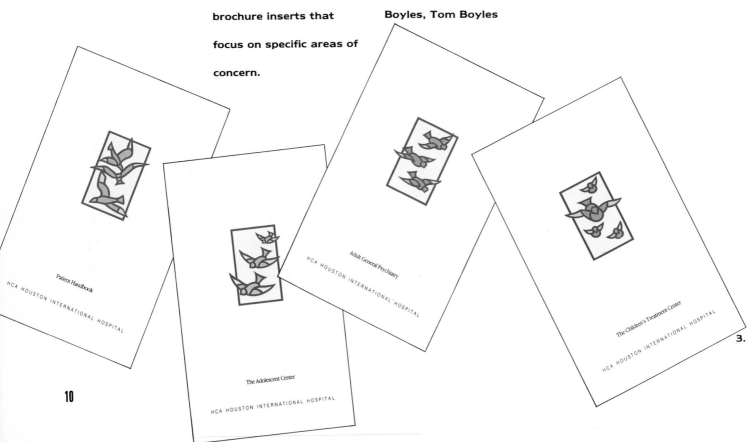

Patient Handbook
HCA HOUSTON INTERNATIONAL HOSPITAL

The Adolescent Center
HCA HOUSTON INTERNATIONAL HOSPITAL

Adult General Psychiatry
HCA HOUSTON INTERNATIONAL HOSPITAL

The Children's Treatment Center
HCA HOUSTON INTERNATIONAL HOSPITAL

3.

1.

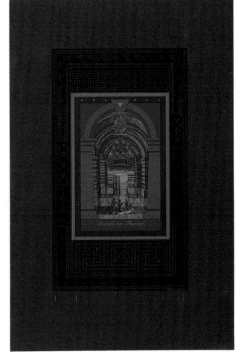

2.

Cover (2) and spreads
(1,3) from promotional
brochure used as a sales
tool and a direct-mail
piece.

**DESIGN FIRM: Sibley/
Peteet Design, Dallas,
Texas**

DESIGNER: Rex Peteet

3.

James River

Paper products

1.

2.

Westinghouse Electric

Nuclear and advanced technology

5.

3.

4.

Spot illustrations (1,2,3,4) and interior spread (5) from foldout employee incentive brochure promoting company's "Total Quality: A journey not a destination" program.

DESIGNERS: Rich and Jody Harydzak/ Westinghouse Energy Systems, Pittsburgh, Pennsylvania
ILLUSTRATOR: Rich Harydzak

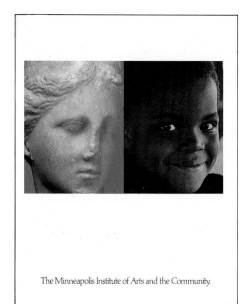

The Minneapolis Institute of Arts and the Community.

1.

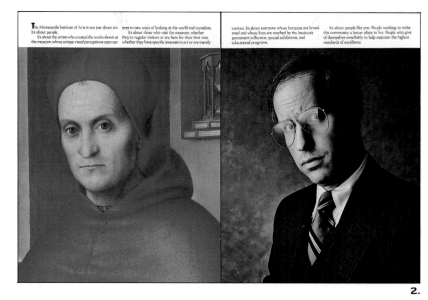

The Minneapolis Institute of Arts is not just about art. It's about people. It's about the artists who created the works shown at the museum, whose unique visual perceptions open our eyes to new ways of looking at the world and ourselves. It's about those who visit the museum, whether they're regular visitors or are here for their first visit, whether they have specific interests in art or are merely curious. It's about everyone whose horizons are broadened and whose lives are touched by the Institute's permanent collection, special exhibitions, and educational programs. It's about people like you. People working to make this community a better place to live. People who give of themselves unselfishly to help maintain the highest standards of excellence.

2.

Reaching Out With Innovative Programs To attract new visitors and families, we've developed a program called Discovery Tours. Each tour focuses on a single topic of general interest, such as wild animals, fantastic creatures, love, ships, and so forth, and shows visitors how that topic is reflected in the works of artists from different times and cultures. This year, another pilot program was developed to reach into inner city neighborhoods. Called the Paper Tigers project, it's a cooperative program developed with the Minneapolis Park and Recreation Board. Paper Tigers is designed to help children of all ages discover the artist in themselves. Children learn how to make paper right in their neighborhood parks and then are brought to the Institute for a visit. Afterwards, they create their own work of art.

3.

The Minneapolis Institute of Arts

Museum

Cover (1) and spreads (2,3) from promotional leave-behind brochure used by representatives calling on corporate donors.

DESIGN FIRM: Chuck Ruhr Advertising, Minneapolis, Minnesota

ART DIRECTOR:

Randy Hughes

COPYWRITER:

Bill Johnson

ALLEY THEATRE

1.

Cover (1), spreads (2,3)

and spot photos (4) from

fundraising brochure

directed at Houston's

corporate community.

DESIGN FIRM: Lowell

Williams Design,

Houston, Texas

ART DIRECTOR/

DESIGNER:

Lowell Williams

DESIGNER: Bill Carson

PHOTOGRAPHER:

Terry Vine

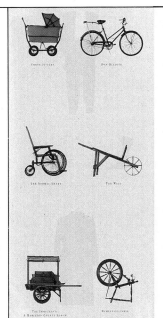

Building On a Legacy. Since its first production in 1947, in a dance studio on Main Street entered from an alleyway, the Alley has built an unsurpassed reputation within American theatre for theatrical innovation, artistic integrity and high professional standards.

Along the way, it has taken risks - from the non-traditional thrust and arena stages to the works appearing on them - and theatre has been made better.

But overall, what's brought the Alley critical renown and success in an arts medium typically fraught with failure has been its constancy as a Producer of quality theatre.

As artistic director of the Alley Theatre, Gregory Boyd views the Alley's ongoing responsibility to Houston, to Texas and to American theatre in straightforward fashion:

Build ambitiously on the Alley's legacy.

The objectives Boyd has set forth emphasize 1) enlarging audience support locally, nationally and internationally with a varied repertoire; 2) expanding audience awareness and understanding of theatre; and 3) extending the Alley's educational outreach programs for young audiences.

2.

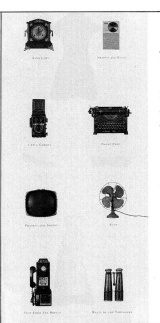

From the Sharp Young Company comes the Traveling Repertory Ensemble Alley Theatre, or TREAT. Each year TREAT tours area schools, hospitals and other social service organizations, presenting productions appropriate to each.

In addition, the Alley and Sharp Young Company stage a professional production at the Alley to introduce young audiences to the best in theatre and help them understand it as an art form.

The Alley Children's Theatre Program stages an in-house production each June for minority children in day care and other worthwhile organizations, while the Tiny Tim Fund provides tickets to disadvantaged children.

Altogether, through its various children's programs, the Alley reaches an estimated 50,000 youngsters each year.

Helping the Alley Help Itself. On average, Alley Theatre ticket sales contribute 65% of its annual operating budget, well above most performing arts organizations. The remaining 35%, however, determines whether the show goes on or not. It's this margin of difference the Alley must find anew each year.

In addition to pursuing aid from the National Endowment for the Arts, the Texas Commission on the Arts and the Cultural Arts Council of Houston, the Alley has tailored a fund-raising program for corporations, foundations and individuals to

3.

4.

ORPHANS   WALTZ OF THE TOREADORS   ALL MY SONS   THE LAST FLAPPER   THE MISER   VOICE OF THE PRAIRIE

Virginia Grown Vegetables

1.

Virginia Grown Fruits

2.

Virginia Department of Agriculture

State agency

Covers (1,2,3,4) and information sheets (5) from booklets used to promote agricultural products from Virginia.

DESIGN FIRM/AGENCY:

Peter Wong & Associates, Richmond, Virginia

ART DIRECTOR/ DESIGNER: Tom Hale

DESIGNER: Dana Cutright

ILLUSTRATOR: Lynn Blakemore

Virginia Grown Broccoli

Features & Benefits: Virginia growers use a modern slurry-ice system to keep broccoli fresh from farm to produce department. Slurry ice, an ice and water mixture, is poured over broccoli as it is packed. The broccoli is then put on refrigerated trucks headed for buyers in major markets.

Virginia broccoli is easily recognized by its fresh bluish-green color and its tight heads.

To meet high packing standards, Virginia broccoli is inspected, assuring that, in addition to being decay or disease free, it has no flowering heads, ice packing and proximity to major markets ensure

that Virginia broccoli arrives fresh and maintains a long shelf life.

Variety: Green Duke, Premium Crop, Gem

Pack Size: Box (25 lbs.)

Grade: U.S. No. 1

Trends: Virginia broccoli acreage is expected to show a small increase in 1989. Demand for Virginia produced broccoli is high. The upper limits on the amount of Virginia broccoli which can be marketed at a profit is great. Broccoli acreage increased with the creation of the Southside Virginia Produce cooperative.

BROCCOLI	MAY	JUNE	JULY	AUG	SEPT	OCT	NOV	DEC

5.

Virginia Grown Peanuts

Virginia Poultry

Virginia Grown Peanuts

Variety: NC 7, Florigiani, NC 6

Pack size: Pound, two pound, bulk, etc.

Grade: U.S. Jumbo Handpicked, U.S. Fancy Handpicked

Trends: Peanut yield per acre over the past five years has averaged approximately 2,900 pounds. Yield per acre

over the past five years has been within, plus or minus, 200 pounds of the five-year average yield per acre for the peanut crop. The average 1989-90 crop year, assuming normal growing conditions, is estimated at 2,985 pounds per acre. Peanut yield forecast for 1989-90 is slightly higher than the average yield of the past five years.

Peanut production in Virginia over the past five years has ranged from a low of 245 million pounds in 1987 to a high of approximately 284 million pounds in 1985. Peanut production over the past five years has fluctuated moderately. Average peanut production since 1984 has been approximately 271 million pounds. Peanut production for 1989-90 crop year is expected to be approximately 271 million pounds. The 8 million pounds above production than in 1988-89, but 3 million pounds above the average peanut production of the past five years.

countries.

extra bonus from as their nutritional es. They are cholesterol-free and high in protein.

Virginia Chick

Classification: Broiler fryer, broiler breaster, with or without giblets.

Products: Fresh or frozen. Whole, cut up and specialty, including deli. Also fresh, frozen or cooked chicken parts in tray pack, cry-o-vac and microwavable.

Packaging: Wide variety of pack sizes. Bulk and individual packaging is available for institutional, fast-food and consumer use.

Grade: Federal, state grade and plant grade available.

Features and Benefits: Virginia has a well established industry. Major national processors in Virginia contract with individual producers throughout the state, result ing in an abundant supply to meet industry needs for large orders as well as small orders. Produced under controlled environment with

routine health inspections under state guidelines. Poultry meets USDA and industry guidelines for health and wholesomeness. The Virginia poultry industry maintains a separate laboratory maintains a res both state and federal facilities to assure the highest quality products are available.

Availability: Fresh, frozen, whole or cut-up, year-round.

Weight price labeling is available. Product is ready for display.

Virginia Grown Apples

Features & Benefits: Virginia has an apple for every reason and every season. Eight major apple varieties are grown in Virginia, and each variety has its own unique characteristics.

Virginia's Red and Golden Delicious varieties are the all-time favorites for out-of-hand eating. In addition, our Red Delicious apples generally are crisper and juicier than apples from most other apple producing areas in the U.S.A. Virginia's York, Winesap, Rome, Jonathan, Stayman and Granny Smith apples are good for baking, frying, making apple juice and applesauce, as well as out-of-hand eating.

Because of their proximity to major markets Virginia apples are more economical to transport year-round and nearly make Virginia one of the top apple-producing states in the nation.

Pack Size: Box (42 pounds), Tray Pack, Bulk, Consumer Bags

Grade: Tray Pack: U.S. Extra Fancy, VA Extra Fancy (Red Color), Combination (Red Sport Varieties 90% U.S. Fancy). Combination U.S. Fancy, VA Extra Fancy, U.S. Fancy, Virginia Fancy, Bags: U.S. Extra Fancy, Combination U.S. Extra and U.S. Fancy, U.S. Fancy

Variety: Red Delicious, Golden Delicious, Rome, Stayman, York, Winesap, Granny Smith, Jonathan

Trends: Apple production in Virginia since 1984 has ranged from a low of 595 million pounds in 1985 to a high of 481 million pounds in 1987. On average, apple production in Virginia is about 400-465 million pounds. Virginia apple production is forecasted at 464.5 million pounds in 1989. The latest Virginia apple and peach tree survey done in orchards, have increased a number, have increased to 1%. The use of dwarf, semi-dwarf and spur-type trees continued to climb. These rootstocks comprised 57% of all trees in 1987, compared with 50% in 1982.

	SEPT	OCT	NOV	DEC	JAN	FEB	MAR	APR	MAY
RED DELICIOUS									
GOLDEN DELICIOUS									
ROME									
STAYMAN									
YORK									
WINESAP									
GRANNY SMITH									
JONATHAN									

CONTROLLED ATMOSPHERE STORAGE
REGULAR STORAGE

	JAN	FEB	MAR	APR	MAY	JUN	JUL
PEANUTS							

1.

2.

3.

4.

The Science Museum of Minnesota

Museum

Cover (1), spreads (2,4) and spot photo (3) from fundraising brochure designed to communicate the excitement in experiencing the museum.

DESIGN FIRM: Avchen & Associates, Inc., Minneapolis, Minnesota

ART DIRECTOR/ DESIGNER: Leslee Avchen

DESIGNER: Laurie Jacobi

PHOTOGRAPHERS: Judy Olausen (portrait), Rick Bell (objects)

COPYWRITERS: Caroline Hall Otis, Paul Mohrbacher

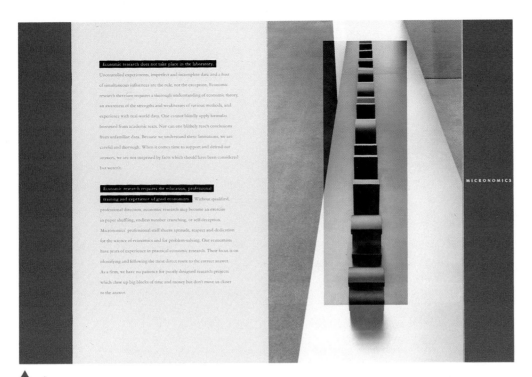

Spreads from capabilities brochure.

DESIGN FIRM: Cross Associates, A Siegel & Gale Company, Los Angeles, California

ART DIRECTOR: James Cross

DESIGNERS: Yee-Ping Cho, Joseph Jacquez

PHOTOGRAPHER: Rick Ueda

Micronomics

Economic research

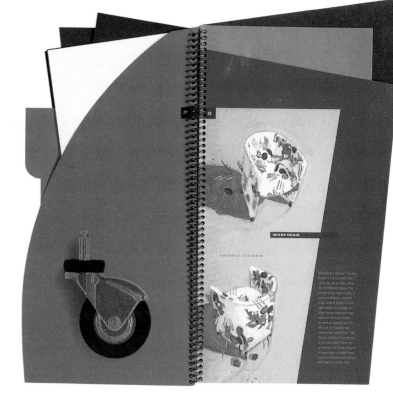

Spreads from
promotional sales
brochure.
DESIGN FIRM: Cross
Associates, Los Angeles,
California
DESIGNER: Ken Cook
PHOTOGRAPHER:
Henrik Kam
ILLUSTRATORS:
Steve Lyons, Sheldon
Greenburg

Simpson Paper

Paper products

Spread (1), cover (2) and

illustration (3) from

capabilities brochure.

DESIGN FIRM: Kenney

Advertising Group,

Minneapolis, Minnesota

ART DIRECTOR:

Brooke Kenney

ILLUSTRATOR:

Stan Olson

COPYWRITER:

Harry Beckwith

You've gotta know this territory.
(Beware, it's flooded.)

1.

Automated Communications

Market research

"Say, how many sales people work for your company?"

"Ohhh. About half of 'em."

How to find more people to sell to. And sell more of the people you find.

2.

3.

1.

Entering the
21st Century

2.

Wadsworth Atheneum

Art museum

"A new set
of sensations
into the world"

Sol LeWitt
American, born 1928
Untitled, 1988
Painted wood
Gift of Sol and Carol LeWitt,
given in memory of
Nellie and Bella LeWitt

"At the thought of Sol LeWitt and his
work, a pervasive well-being comes
over me. I know that a new work by
him, whether very large or quite small,
is likely to bend space in a new way,
give forms of every kind a new identity
and work with a gamut of color that
is never blatant.

"In-between color, one might call it, for
it takes color in its raw, hot-and-strong
state and subjects it to combinations
and readjustments that never fight for
our attention. It is, in fact, on a
chromatic middle ground that his color
comes to fruition.

"On the actual site, LeWitt himself
neither draws nor paints. The hands
that make the work are the hands of
others. He has the idea, and he writes
it down; and others do the work.

"Teamwork is essential. Trust is fundamental. As the work proceeds, a sense
of shared glory comes over the team
members. But glory, in this context,
has nothing to do with vainglory. The
annihilation of self, in the work, leads
to a sense of collective harmony. And
when they're all done, that collective
harmony is there for all of us to share.

"As to where we should place LeWitt's
work in any given hierarchy of yesterday or today, I don't know. I don't care,
either. Art is not about listings. It is
about the very few people who can
bring a new set of sensations into the
world. Sol LeWitt is one of them."

John Russell

John Russell
Art Critic, The New York Times

20

Contemporary Art:
The Best of the New

Contemporary art challenges the
viewer, as well as the museum world:
out of the bewildering variety of
new movements and works, which
will endure?

Some institutions avoid the question
by waiting until the new has become
old. The Atheneum chooses to exhibit
a variety of new work, apply rigorous
judgment and acquire work that merits
the risk of acquisition. Obviously, such
artistic activism means showing con-
troversial work. The Atheneum seeks
to encourage innovation, uphold artistic freedom and investigate the most
promising new departures.

The Wadsworth Atheneum's contem-
porary collection ranges from the
masters of Abstract Expressionism who
shifted the center of Western art from
Paris to New York — Jackson Pollock,
Willem de Kooning, Mark Rothko,
Franz Kline and others — to their
notable heirs — Robert Rauschenberg,
Andy Warhol, Donald Judd and
Sol LeWitt — to the work of African-
American artists such as Romare
Bearden and Bob Thompson.

The Atheneum's widely-respected
MATRIX Gallery has been a showcase
since 1975 of the newest work of such
leading-edge artists as Robert
Mapplethorpe, the Starn Twins and
Annette Lemieux.

4.

Wadsworth Atheneum

Of the World,
For the City

3.

Covers (2,3) and spreads (4,5) from promotional brochures for capital campaign; cover of slipcase (1) containing the two brochures.

DESIGN FIRM: Peter Good Graphic Design, Chester, Connecticut

ART DIRECTOR/ DESIGNER: Peter Good

ART DIRECTOR: Susan Fasick-Jones

PHOTOGRAPHER: Rob Lisak

"The revelation is one of Ernst's most memorable"

Max Ernst
German, 1960–1976
Europe after the Rain, 1940-42
Oil on canvas
The Ella Gallup Sumner and
Mary Catlin Sumner Collection

"*Europe after the Rain* was bought for the Wadsworth Atheneum by Chick Austin in the year it was finished, 1942. The Atheneum's association with Surrealism, however, was not new. As early as 1931, the Atheneum had presented the first survey of Surrealist art, which, of course, included Max Ernst.

"Throughout his long career, Ernst explored and exploited many 'unortho-dox' methods of painting and drawing. For *Europe after the Rain*, he first squashed wet pigments of paint across the canvas. The resulting decalco-mania looked like a sponge, porous and thirsty. Its flat surface suggested to Ernst definite forms and shapes, and these he defined by partially painting over the decalcomania and by detailing further accidents of its impression. The blue sky that covers the underlying decalcomania silhouettes the remaining landscape from which Ernst conjures hidden phantoms.

"Ernst began *Europe after the Rain* in 1940 in France. The next year, with the help of a few friends, he escaped Europe and found refuge in the United States. The Atheneum painting, a wide panorama, describes in allegory his displacements and exile. The revelation is one of Ernst's most memorable. It is also his most important later work, and its desolate and disturbing image reflects conditions of our anxious time."

William S. Lieberman

William S. Lieberman
Chairman, Department of 20th-Century Art,
The Metropolitan Museum of Art

Modern Art:
The Astonishment of
Genius at Play

The voice of 20th-century art was new and startling. Once again, the Atheneum was in the lead, acquiring important works by Picasso, being the first museum in the country to own a Mondrian, introducing Salvador Dali to America. The museum's 20th-century American collection includes work from the important movements — from the socially minded Ashcan School painting of John Sloan to the cool jazz of Stuart Davis to the natural sensuousness of Georgia O'Keeffe.

When Surrealism burst upon the scene in the 1920s, most people inside and outside of the art establishment were bewildered, shocked and repelled — as they were meant to be. Surrealism's bizarre juxtaposition of meticulous artistry and nightmarish subject matter still strikes with tremendous force today. Its effect in the twenties was almost terrorizing.

The Atheneum was the first American museum to acquire major paintings by Joan Miro, Salvador Dali and Max Ernst — many of them bought in the year they were painted — and today offers one of the finest anthologies of Surrealist painting in the United States.

16

5.

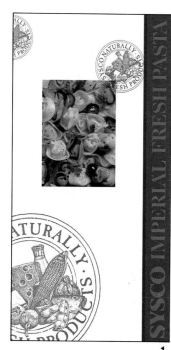

Cover (1), closed gatefold (2) and open gatefold (3) of promotional brochure.

DESIGN FIRM: Adcetera Design Studio, Houston, Texas

DESIGNERS: Kristy Sexton, Becky Walker

PHOTOGRAPHER: Ralph Smith

1.

2.

Sysco Foods

Food products

3.

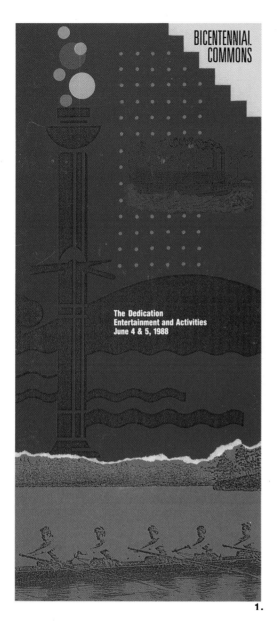

1.

3.

2.

Cover (1) and spreads (2,3) from souvenir booklet for a park built to commemorate the bicentennial.

DESIGN FIRM: George Tassian Organization, Covington, Kentucky
ART DIRECTORS: Sherry Rogers, Kelly Kolar
DESIGNER: Sherry Rogers

Paper products

September may be the ninth month of the year, but all the same it is a time for beginnings. The school year starts; so does the football season, the fall TV schedule, the eating of oysters and the Jewish New Year. Indeed, the origins of eight percent of everything on earth can be traced to the month of September: chop suey (1896), the city of Los Angeles (1781), General Motors (1908), The New York Times (1851), Mickey Mouse (1928), the 'Star-Spangled Banner' (1814), the nickname 'Uncle Sam' (1813), and carpet sweepers (1876). They were all concocted, established, founded, published, born, composed, thought up or patented in the month of September. September isn't the end of the year, but even so it is a time for endings – the lease on the cottage by the lake, for example, the regular baseball season, reruns on TV, the eating of fresh corn, summer and the slathering-on of sunscreen. In years past, September has been the end of the line for George Washington (1796),

William McKinley (1901), Nathan Hale (1775), Huey Long (1935), John L. Sullivan (1892), child labor (1916), the old city of London (1666) and the Japanese in World War II (1945). George Washington gave his Farewell Address in September, the others were assassinated, hanged, shot, KO'd, prohibited, burned and defeated, in that order. September is a time for putting certain things into the ground and for taking others out. We plant spinach, lettuce, radishes, winter wheat and celery. We harvest squash, pumpkins, apples, grapes, brussel sprouts, kale, peppers, cranberries and collards. In September, birds begin their southward migration, following the sun as it slips below the equator and brings summer to the southern hemisphere. Meanwhile, up in our neck of the woods, deciduous trees turn brilliant autumn colors, mornings and evenings become chilly, and once again the nights grow longer than the days.

1.

September 1988: Walleye Tournament, New Glarus, Wisconsin

September 1901: President William McKinley shot in Buffalo, New York

2.

September 1936: Buddy Holly born

September 1916: Emergency Revenue Act doubles the rate of income tax

3.

The waters of Lake Superior rise to their highest level in September.

4.

A Month of Days from Mead and Gilbert Papers

5.

Cover (5) and spreads (1,2,3,4) from promotional brochure.

DESIGN FIRM:

Pentagram Design, New York, New York

ART DIRECTOR:

Peter Harrison

ART DIRECTOR/ DESIGNER:

Susan Hochbaum

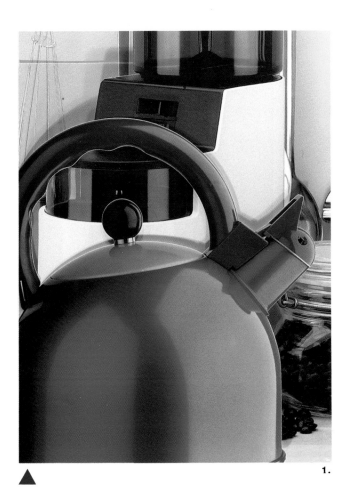

1.

Cover (1) and inside front cover (2) from announcement and exhibitor application for "Accent on Housewares" exhibition.

DESIGN FIRM:

E.B. Wilson, New York, New York

ART DIRECTOR:

Allan Bealy

PHOTOGRAPHER:

Truman Moore

Now there's an exciting, exclusive marketplace in New York City where you can reach influential retailers and decision-makers in the powerful housewares and gourmet industries. Presenting Accent on Housewares. .

Accent on Housewares is a unique forum for manufacturers of distinctive kitchen, gourmet and housewares products. And it's designed to address the needs of the industry for a fall exhibit.

Whether you specialize in small appliances, bakeware, cookware, cutlery, gadgets or home textiles, here's your opportunity to meet face to face with the housewares buyers who mean business in one of the largest retail markets in the country. Accent

2.

George Little Management

Exhibit management

The relationship of an invention to society is a puzzle. RCT is the world's leading authority in pulling together and joining all of the pieces. Contact RCT and let us tell you how we can work together to insure that inventions are identified and commercialized for the benefit not only of your institution, but of our technology-based industries and local, state and national economies.

1.

We've Created the Future Before.

2.

3.

Research Corporation Technologies

Identifies, evaluates, protects, invests in and commercializes inventions

Cover (2) and spreads (1,3) from capabilities brochure.

DESIGN FIRM: Hubbard & Hubbard Design, Phoenix, Arizona

ART DIRECTOR/ DESIGNER: Ann Morton Hubbard

ILLUSTRATORS: Dale Verzaal, Michael Swaine, Arnold Roth, Alan Ganres, M.C. Escher, Brian Karas, Curtis Parker

1.

2.

3.

Goldsmith, Agio & Company

Investment banking

Cover (1), spreads (2,3)
and spot illustration (4)
from capabilities
brochure.
DESIGN FIRM: Charles S.
Anderson Design
Company, Minneapolis,
Minnesota

ART DIRECTOR/
DESIGNER: Dan Olson
PHOTOGRAPHERS; Joel
Baldwin, Thomas Lea,
Charles Thatcher, Greg
Pease, Steve Brady
COPYWRITER:
Jon Anderson

4.

Printing/lithography

Envelope (1), cover (2) and spreads (3,4,5,6) from capabilities brochure.

DESIGN FIRM: Frazier Design, San Francisco, California

1.

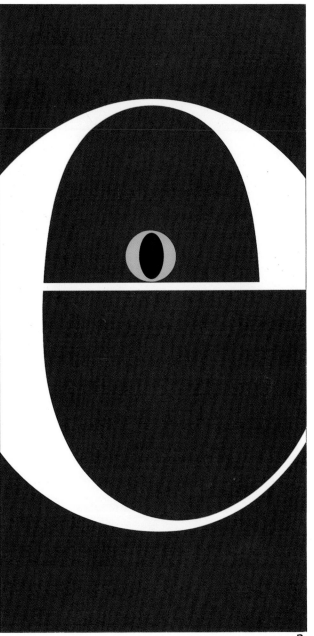

2.

ART DIRECTOR/

DESIGNER: Craig Frazier

DESIGNER:

Darrel Kolosta

PHOTOGRAPHER:

Rudi Legname

COPYWRITER:

Greg Karraker

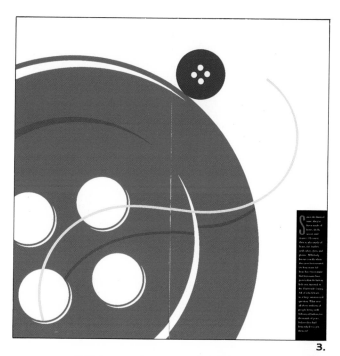

3.

4.

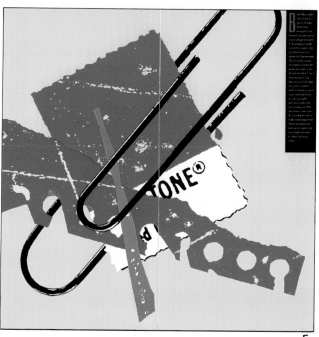

5.

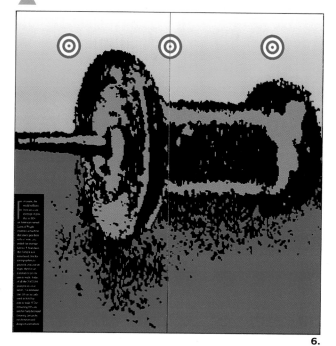

6.

Cover (1), spreads (2,3) and typographic detail (4) from brochure, directed at the graphic design community, promoting use of Simpson papers in annual reports.

Simpson Paper

Paper products

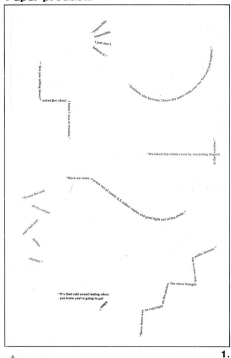

1.

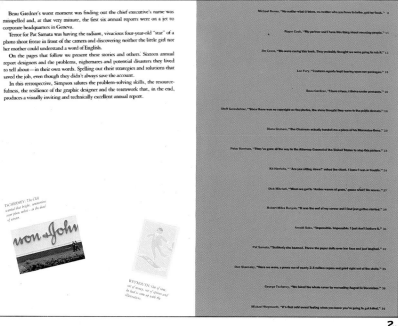

2.

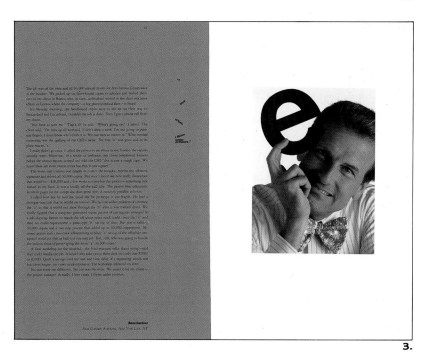

3.

ART DIRECTORS/
DESIGNERS: Roger Cook,
Don Shanosky
DESIGNER:
Robert Frankle
PORTRAIT
PHOTOGRAPHER:
Carlos Eguiguren
COPYWRITER:
Chris Barnett
DESIGN FIRM: Cook and
Shanosky, Princeton,
New Jersey

4. "Since there was no copyright on the photos, the store thought they were in the public domain."

Be Pre-peared.

1.

Cover (1) and interior spread (3) from capabilities foldout piece introducing new company logo (2).

DESIGN FIRM: Trousdell Design, Atlanta, Georgia

DESIGNERS: Don and Tina Trousdell

COVER PAINTING: Doug Montross

ILLUSTRATORS: Will Crowther (rabbit), Paul Blakey (pear)

PHOTOGRAPHER: Gin Ellis

COPYWRITER: Rich Maender

PERRY COMMUNICATIONS, INC.

2.

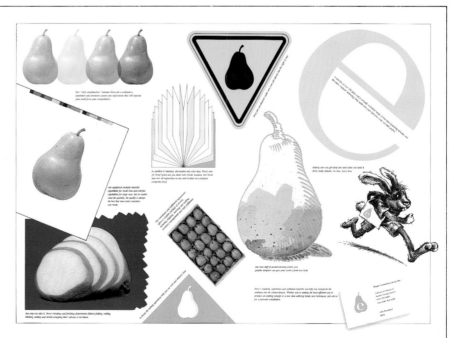

3.

Perry Communications
Printing

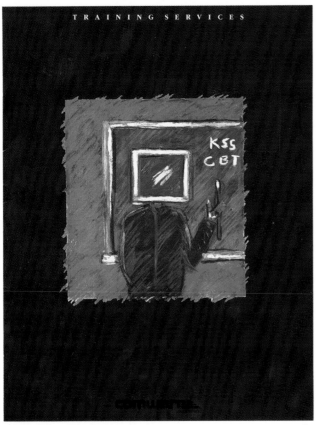

1.

2.

5.

6.

Comware

Computer software

REFERENCE SERVICES

3.

4.

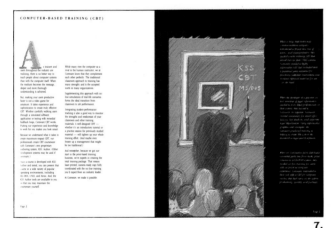

7.

Covers (1,2,3,4), spreads
(5,6,7) and illustration
(8) from series of
capabilities brochures.

ART DIRECTOR: Patricia
Holtel/Comware, Inc.,
Cincinnati, Ohio
ILLUSTRATOR:
Sondra Bakie

8.

International Printing

Printing

Cover (1), spreads (2,3)
and spot illustration (4)
from promotional
brochure focusing on
client testimonials.

DESIGN FIRM: George
Kubas II Design,
Lakewood, Ohio

**ART DIRECTOR/
DESIGNER:**
George Kubas II

PHOTOGRAPHER:
Andrew Russetti

COPYWRITER: Bill Glover

2.

3.

1.

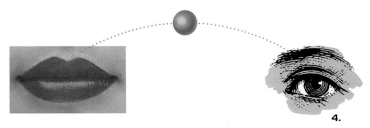

4.

SEX: BEING READY AND THE PILL

Deciding when you're ready for sex is a very personal decision. There's lots to consider. If you stay in control of your sex life, it can be a beautiful and rewarding experience. If you lose control and get pregnant when you don't want to be, you can end up having a miserable time—for a long time. An unplanned pregnancy can ruin your plans for the future.

ADMITTING WE HAVE SEX

Why don't more of us use birth control? One reason is that a lot of us don't like admitting that we have sex. We tell ourselves we're not going to have sex—then we have it. After we have it, we tell ourselves we'll never do it again—then we do. Why would we rather gamble with pregnancy than admit we have sex? There are lots of reasons.

Lots of us feel guilty about having sex. We fool ourselves into thinking that sex is beyond our control. We think we can avoid feeling guilty if we don't admit that we're going to have sex. When it comes to birth control, we'd rather take our chances than be prepared. We let our guilt confuse us.

1.

2.

Cover (2), spreads (1,3) and spot illustation (4) for informational pamphlet on forms of birth control.

DESIGN FIRM: Belk Mignogna Associates

ART DIRECTOR: Howard Belk

DESIGNER: Carin Berger

ILLUSTRATOR: Arlen Schumer/The Dynamic Duo Studio, Inc., New York, New York

have seven placebo or fake pills that are a different color. You take these when you have your period to stay in the habit of taking the Pill every day. Taking the Pill at the same time every day helps increase its effectiveness and makes it easier to remember to take it. If you forget to take a pill, take it as soon as you remember, even if it means taking two the next day. If you forget more than one pill per cycle, consult your physician. In addition, use another form of birth control for the remainder of that month.

Follow your doctor's instructions and the instructions on the package exactly.

PREGNANCY AND THE PILL

When you want to become pregnant, stop taking the Pill and use another form of birth control while you wait for your period to become regular. Taking the Pill while you're pregnant increases the risks of defects in the developing fetus. After giving birth, ask your doctor when you can take the Pill again.

Even if you take the Pill on schedule every day, there is a very small chance of pregnancy. So, if you haven't skipped any pills and your period doesn't come twice in a row, it is very important to see your doctor.

BIRTH CONTROL CAN HELP US ENJOY SEX

IT'S NOT SO EMBARRASSING

SO I TOLD HER, CHILL OUT! TAKING THE PILL IS NO BIG DEAL. AND IT DOESN'T MAKE ME FEEL CHEAP,... IN FACT, IT MAKES ME FEEL SAFE!

3.

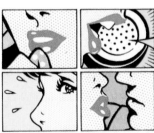

4.

Lexis Pharmaceuticals
Pharmaceuticals

PHH Fleet America

Truck fleet management

PHH FleetAmerica

PHH

1.

PHH FleetAmerica

Fleet

Administration

2.

Cover (1) and one of a series of inserts (2) from sales/marketing kit explaining company services.

DESIGN FIRM:

R.S. Jensen, Baltimore, Maryland

ART DIRECTOR/ DESIGNER:

Robert Shelley

DESIGNER:

Robert Rytter

PHOTOGRAPHER:

Phil Branner

Cover (1) and interior (2) of promotional folder for an Australian real estate company.

DESIGN FIRM: Josh Freeman Associates, Los Angeles, California

ART DIRECTORS: Josh Freeman, Greg Clarke

DESIGNERS: Greg Clarke, Vickie Sawyer Karten

ILLUSTRATOR: Greg Clarke

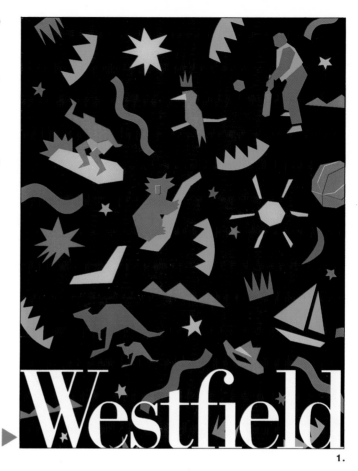

1.

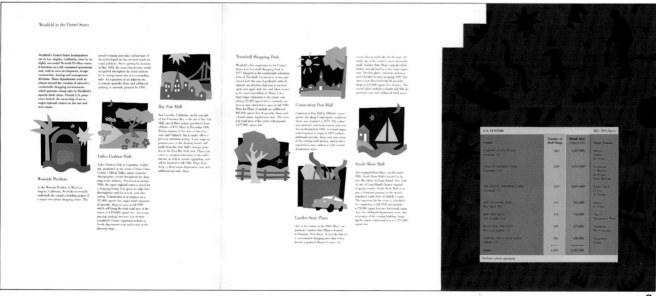

2.

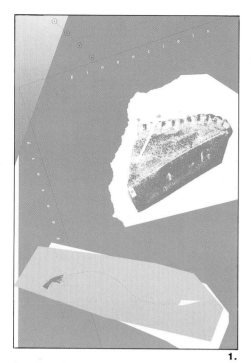

1.

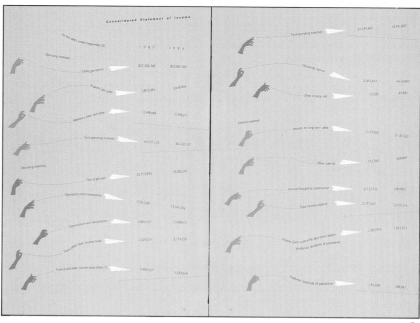

2.

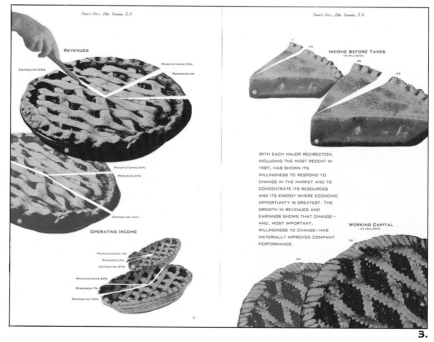

3.

Cover (1) and spreads
(2,3) from promotional
sales brochure.

DESIGN FIRM:
Weymouth Design,
Boston, Massachusetts
ART DIRECTOR:
Michael Weymouth
DESIGNER: Jose Lizardo

Monadnock Paper Mills
Paper products

Cover (1) and spread (2)
from promotional
brochure on the subject
of food.

DESIGN FIRM:
Yamamoto Moss,
Minneapolis, Minnesota
DESIGNERS: Hideki
Yamamoto, Miranda
Moss
PHOTOGRAPHY:
Marvy! Advertising
Photography, Hopkins,
Minnesota (1), Michael
Jensen (2)

1.

Consolidated Papers

Paper products

2.

1.

Cover (1) and spread (5) from direct response mailer for family concert series; covers (2,3,4) of brochures for individual concerts in series.
DESIGN FIRM: Peter Good Graphic Design, Chester, Connecticut
DESIGNER/ ILLUSTRATOR: Peter Good

Hartford Symphony Orchestra

Music

Music in Space

Meet the Orchestra

Pictures at an Exhibition

2.

3.

Three Saturday matinees of music & fun for the whole family featuring the Hartford Symphony Orchestra conducted by Michael Lankester. All concerts begin at 11:00 a.m. at The Bushnell and last about an hour.

4.

5.

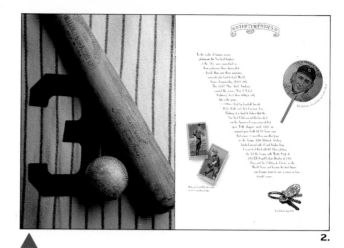

1.

2.

3.

4.

5.

Consolidated Paper

Paper products

Cover (5) and spreads (1,2,3,4) from promotional sales brochure featuring baseball.

DESIGN FIRM: Avchen & Associates, Inc., Minneapolis, Minnesota

ART DIRECTOR: Leslee Avchen

DESIGNERS: Leslee Avchen, Laurie Jacobi

ILLUSTRATORS: Leslee Avchen, Laurie Jacobi, John Vasiliou

FINISHED COMPUTER ART: Jon Poor

COPYWRITING: Cindy Zwirn

When you consider the enormous structural changes taking place in the global economy, it seems only natural that new corporate strategies and management principles will evolve.

And since management success has always been measured by the ability to optimize corporate resources, we feel the time is right to reassess which of those will be most important to develop in the volatile, dynamic, new marketplace.

Historically, corporate resources have been natural resources or capital assets. Currently, the power of the microchip has captured the imagination of corporate leaders. And we believe the focus is beginning to shift again: this time the primary emphasis will be on human resources.

This shift is resulting from the emergence of services and industries not even imaginable a decade ago that are changing our economic landscape: new professional services, high technology firms, and information-processing companies. All are facing the same major challenge for success—the need to have informed, knowledgeable, and creative people.

To compete successfully in the long run, companies will need a vision that enables employees to approach their jobs differently from the way they did in the manufacturing or industrial age.

Ironically, while technological advances in recent years have been unparalleled, corporate leaders are still struggling to create environments which enable individuals to

Making the future happen depends on more than foresight; it also calls for a deep insight into the limitations and possibilities of the organization as it exists today.

Our focus is to help corporate leaders fully integrate the development of employees into a productive long-term strategy.

Most strategic planning efforts tend to downplay the people dimension. In the new economy, neglecting this critical area can spell the difference between success and failure.

Working with whatever planning efforts are already underway, we help clarify an organization's strategic vision by developing a "blueprint" for mastering the people challenges that lie ahead.

A well-prepared strategic human resources plan can produce the following results: ● define future leadership needs ● identify critical skills and resource areas ● design jobs to more effectively meet upcoming challenges ● uncover each employee's potential, and identify sources of tomorrow's talent ● devise measurement systems for the attainment of individual and organizational goals ● create opportunities for individual growth that coincide with the evolving needs of the corporation.

We have found that such a blueprint is most effective when integrated into the corporation's strategic plan. Very few organizations, however, have managed to do this successfully on their own.

● One of the major challenges faced by corporate leaders is bridging the gap between where their organization can go in the future and where it is today.

Making the future happen depends on more than foresight; it also calls for a deep insight into the limitations and possibilities of the organization as it exists today.

We help clarify the organization's strategic vision by developing a "blueprint" for the people challenges that lie ahead.

Spreads from corporate capabilities brochure.
DESIGN FIRM: Cook and Shanosky Associates, Inc., Princeton, New Jersey
ART DIRECTORS/ DESIGNERS: Roger Cook, Dan Shanosky
DESIGNERS: Denise Pollack
PHOTOGRAPHY: Cook and Shanosky Associates, Inc.

Caliper
Management consulting

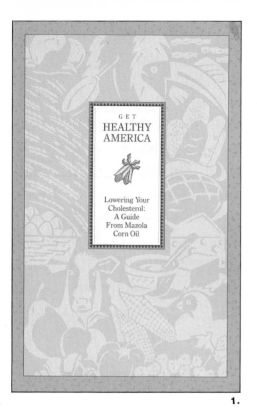

1.

Lower Your Cholesterol Lowering your cholesterol levels does not mean eating less food or boring meals. These two meal plans, both filled with tasty foods, have similar amounts of calories, but differ greatly in cholesterol and saturated fat content. And the lower-fat meal plan lets you eat a wider variety of delicious foods.

	Typical American Diet	Lower-fat Diet
Breakfast	1 fried egg 2 strips crisp bacon 2 slices white toast with 1 tsp butter 1 cup orange juice Black coffee or tea	1 cup bran cereal with ½ cup blueberries 1 cup 1% low-fat milk 1 cup orange juice Black coffee or tea
Snack	1 doughnut (glazed)	1 toasted English muffin with 1 tsp corn oil margarine
Lunch	2 oz salami 1 oz American cheese 2 slices white bread 1 tsp mustard 1 large chocolate chip cookie	3 oz white turkey meat 2 slices whole wheat bread 1 slice tomato 2 tsp real mayonnaise 1 medium apple
Snack	1 oz potato chips (small bag)	2 cups popcorn with 2 tsp melted corn oil margarine
Dinner	3 oz fried hamburger with 1 tbsp ketchup 1 medium baked potato with 1 tbsp sour cream ¾ cup steamed broccoli with 1 tsp butter 1 piece (2 oz) marble cake 12 oz cola	3 oz broiled hamburger with 1 tbsp ketchup 1 medium baked potato with 1 tbsp low-fat yogurt and chives ¾ cup steamed broccoli with 1 tsp corn oil margarine Tossed garden salad with 1 tbsp corn oil and vinegar 1 cup 1% low-fat milk 1 whole wheat roll with 1 tsp corn oil margarine 1 piece (3 oz) gingerbread
Nutritional Information	Calories 2,040 Cholesterol 480mg Total Fat 96g Polyunsaturated Fat 9g Saturated Fat 39g % of calories: Protein 13% Fat 42% Carbohydrate 45%	Calories 2,030 Cholesterol 170mg Total Fat 66g Polyunsaturated Fat 15g Saturated Fat 17g % of calories: Protein 18% Fat 29% Carbohydrate 53%

Basic Food Groups

MEATS, FISH, POULTRY, EGGS, NUTS AND DRIED BEANS

MILK, CHEESES, YOGURTS, ICE CREAM

FRUITS AND VEGETABLES

BREADS, PASTA, CEREALS AND GRAINS

FATS AND OILS

SWEETS AND SNACKS

YOU ARE WHAT YOU EAT

Controlling cholesterol is easiest when it is part of a lifestyle that emphasizes nutrition *and* exercise. The foods you eat are building blocks and fuel for your body.

One of the nice things about eating a lower cholesterol diet is that, in general, it will also lead to weight loss and a healthier diet overall.

To start, eat a balanced variety from each of the basic food groups: shown at left.

Limit serving sizes of rich foods and save treats for special occasions. Moderation, careful meal planning and heart-smart cooking techniques will help in keeping to a realistic, healthful diet.

For example, trimming excess fat from meats, sauteing in corn oil instead of butter and removing skin from poultry will reduce fat intake. Similarly, using low-fat or skim instead of whole milk and substituting corn oil margarine for butter cuts cholesterol. Also, using light corn oil spread instead of butter on bread, rolls, muffins and pancakes is a good way to cut calories.

Fruits and vegetables contain no cholesterol. The same is true for bread, pasta, cereals and other grains. An exception here are commercially-prepared desserts and pastries. Many of these may be high in cholesterol or saturated fat. Also, limit foods which list highly-saturated or hydrogenated oils as one of the first three ingredients.

80/20 Rule: Eating right does not mean completely giving up your favorite foods, even if they are high in cholesterol or saturated fats. A good rule of thumb is the "80-20" rule. It says that if you watch what you eat 80 percent of the time, the other 20 percent is available to treat yourself. If you know you'll be eating a high cholesterol or high-fat meal, try to watch what you eat several meals before and after to balance your diet.

2.

KEEPING A HEALTHFUL KITCHEN

Here's a simple recipe for keeping a healthful kitchen. Start with a nutrition-savvy shopping list, add heart-wise cooking techniques and blend in menu planning.

When creating a healthful kitchen, nothing matters more than the foods you choose. As a first step, become a better shopper. In the supermarket, be aware of prepared foods that contain large amounts of saturated fat and cholesterol. A wide variety of commercially prepared foods may use animal fats as shortenings.

Also be aware of foods containing such vegetable oils as coconut which are high in saturated fat. To do so, it helps to know how to read a simple food label. Be wary of labels that do not specify which vegetable oil is used in the product.

The second step in keeping a healthful kitchen is preparing meals which are lower in saturated fat and cholesterol than traditional family favorites. In menu planning and cooking, look for handy ways of substituting lower-fat ingredients for ones high in fat and cholesterol. This can not only improve your health, but also the taste of some of your favorite dishes.

Reading The Signs
Take time to read package labels to discover important facts about the food inside. By law, when a health or nutrition claim is made on a product's label, information backing that claim must also appear on the package. Information required includes portion size, calories per serving and grams of protein, carbohydrates and fats. Each gram of fat contains about 9 calories, so multiply the grams of fat by 9 to get total calories from fat.

Don't Be Afraid to Fry

AFTER SO MUCH HAS BEEN WRITTEN ABOUT FRYING, MANY PEOPLE MAY FEEL GUILTY ABOUT PREPARING—AND ENJOYING—FRIED FOODS. STIR-FRYING, FOR EXAMPLE, IS AN EASY, TASTY AND NUTRITIOUS WAY OF COOKING, AND EVEN DEEP-FRIED FOODS, WHEN PREPARED PROPERLY IN A POLYUNSATURATED OIL SUCH AS CORN OIL, CAN BE ENJOYED BY MOST PEOPLE IN MODERATION. PAN OR STIR-FRYING IN PURE CORN OR OTHER LIQUID VEGETABLE OILS ADDS NO CHOLESTEROL AND VERY LITTLE SATURATED FATS. THESE ARE VERSATILE COOKING METHODS THAT ARE AT HOME IN ALMOST ANY FOOD.

Good Ways to Cook for Health No matter what you cook, there are a number of simple ways to keep the foods you serve lower in cholesterol and saturated fat. Select lean cuts of beef such as flank steak. Make pot roasts and stews a day ahead. Chill and remove congealed fat. Pan fry with polyunsaturated corn oil rather than butter, lard or bacon fat. Use polyunsaturated corn oil whenever a recipe calls for liquid or melted shortening. Cook roasts, turkey and chicken on a rack so fat can drain off. Remove poultry skin before cooking. Use skim milk and skim milk-based cheeses when recipes call for whole milk cheese. Brown meats and poultry, then pour off fat before continuing with recipe. Prepare vegetables with herbs and a sprinkle of lemon juice instead of cream sauces or butter.

Prepared Foods: Watch What You Eat Don't forget that many prepared foods are rich in saturated fat or cholesterol because of the ingredients they contain. While no food need be completely eliminated from the diet, there are many foods that belong on a go-for-it and go-easy list. Here are just a few:

Go-for-it	Go-easy
Corn oil	Lard, shortening
Margarine	Butter
Homemade popcorn	Taco chips
Pasta with tomato sauce	Canned spaghetti and meat sauce
Peanut butter	Cheese crackers
Sliced turkey	Bologna, salami
Low-fat cottage cheese	American, cheddar cheese
Bread	Commercially-prepared baked goods and pastries
Beans in tomato sauce	Pork and beans
Ice milk, sorbet	Ice cream
Angel food cake	Pound cake with frosting

HeartWise Substitutions
You can make many recipes heart-healthier with these simple ingredient substitutions:

► Rather than butter, use corn oil, corn oil margarine, light corn oil spread
► Rather than whole eggs, use egg whites.
► Rather than greasing baking pans with shortening, use corn oil cooking spray.
► Rather than sour cream, use low-fat yogurt or low-fat cottage cheese.
► Rather than cream cheese, use farmer cheese.
► Rather than whole milk, use skim or low-fat milk.
► Rather than chocolate, use cocoa powder.

3.

Cover (1), spreads (2,3)

and spot illustration (4)

from informational

brochure explaining

cholesterol.

DESIGN FIRM: Patterson

Wood Partners, New

York, New York

DESIGNERS: Tom Wood,

Peg Patterson

ILLUSTRATOR:

Karen Knorr

4.

Best Foods, CPC International
Food products

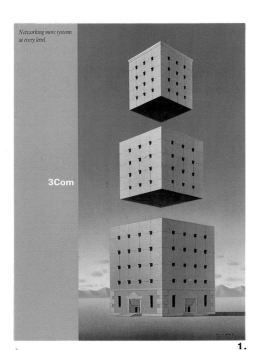

Networking more systems at every level.

3Com

1.

3Com can combine your corporate, departmental, and configuring systems into a single, integrated network.

2.

Cover (1) and spreads

(2,3) from capabilities

brochure.

DESIGN FIRM: Neumeier

Design Team, Atherton,

California

ART DIRECTOR/

DESIGNER:

Marty Neumeier

DESIGNER:

Kathleen Joynes

ILLUSTRATOR:

David Wilcox

3Com can help you build the strategic system that lets your company compete as a unit.

3.

1.

Cover (1) and spreads (2,3) from brochure directed at new and expectant mothers outlining the hospital's obstetrics facilities.

DESIGN FIRM: Knape & Knape, Dallas, Texas

ART DIRECTOR: Willie Baronet

DESIGNER: Kevin Prejean

ILLUSTRATOR: Lynn Rowe Reed

WRITER: Poppy Sundeen

urrounding every pregnancy and birth are all sorts of little matters. Matters that include choosing doctors, classes and birth options. Matters such as the extent of Dad's involvement in the delivery. Matters like provisions for high-risk pregnancies or neonatal intensive care. Matters of who can visit and when. Matters involving preparations for baby's homecoming. Matters enough to make your head spin. That's precisely why we at HCA Medical Center of Plano want you to have this book. It'll help you sort out all those little matters, so that you can concentrate on the biggest little matter of all. Your baby. ▾ ▾ ▾

FATHER'S INVOLVEMENT. There was a time not long ago when conception was the man's major contribution to pregnancy and childbirth. Today, many fathers participate along with their wives and doctors as partners in the childbirth process. At HCA Medical Center of Plano, we make it easier to share the experience by inviting Mom and Dad to take classes together, to

BONDING WITH THE NEW FAMILY MEMBER IS AS IMPORTANT FOR BIG SISTERS, BIG BROTHERS AND GRANDPARENTS AS IT IS FOR MOM AND DAD.

2.

SINCE 1974, THOUSANDS OF LITTLE MATTERS HAVE BEEN BORN HERE. THEY'VE COME IN EVERY SHAPE AND SIZE, LONG AND SHORT, MALE AND FEMALE, BLUE-EYED AND BROWN-EYED, BLONDE, BRUNETTE AND BALD AS AN EGG. BUT VARIED AS THEY ARE, OUR BABIES HAVE ONE THING IN COMMON. ALL ARE CAUSE FOR CELEBRATION BY THEIR FAMILIES AND BY THE STAFF HERE AT HCA MEDICAL CENTER OF PLANO.

3.

1.

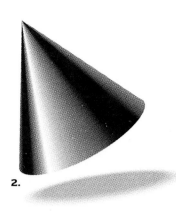

Cover (1), spread (3) and
spot illustration (2) from
computer graphics
capabilities brochure.
**DESIGN FIRM: Kode,
New York, New York
DESIGNER/
ILLUSTRATOR:
William Kochi**

2.

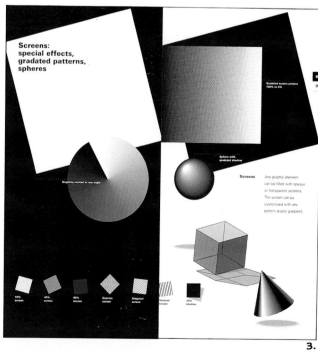

3.

Typogram

Typesetting

1.

Teaser pieces—poster (1), buttons (2), cards and box (5)—from a promotional campaign; spreads (3,4) from hard-cover storybook included in campaign.

DESIGN FIRM: The Duffy Design Group, Minneapolis, Minnesota

ART DIRECTOR/ DESIGNER/ ILLUSTRATOR: Sharon Werner

ILLUSTRATORS: Charles Burns, Lynn Schulte

COPYWRITER: Chuck Carlson

2.

CIRCA 130 GOSSAMER GRAY 80 LB. COVER

3.

CIRCA SELECT PAPRIKA 80 LB. COVER

4.

5.

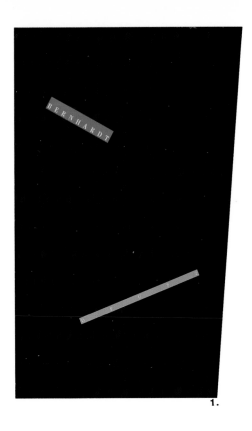

1.

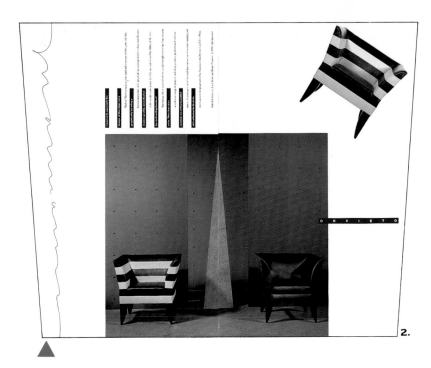

2.

3.

Bernhardt Furniture

Furniture

Cover (1) and spreads
(2,3) from brochure
introducing avant-garde
collection.

DESIGN FIRM: Vanderbyl
Design, San Francisco,
California
DESIGNER:
Michael Vanderbyl

PHOTOGRAPHER:
Ken Litton, Omega
Studios (3)

BCI General Contractors

Commercial construction

Cover (1) and spreads (2,3) from capabilities brochure.

DESIGN FIRM: James Robie Design

ART DIRECTORS: James Robie, Karen Knecht

DESIGNER: Karen Knecht, Long Beach, California

PHOTOGRAPHER: Karen Knauer

2.

3.

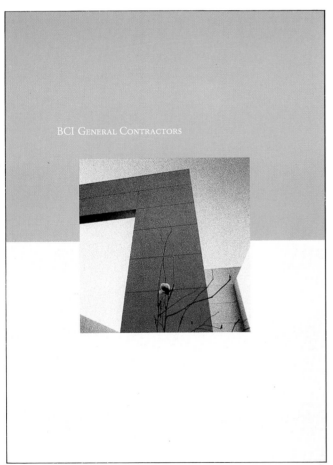

1.

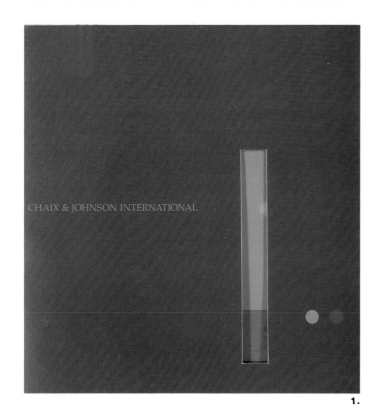

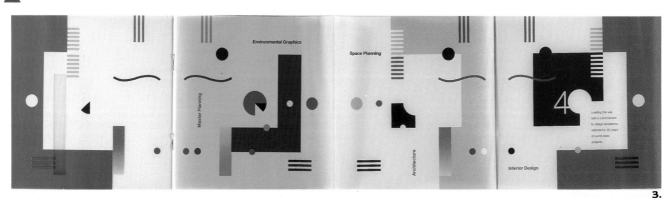

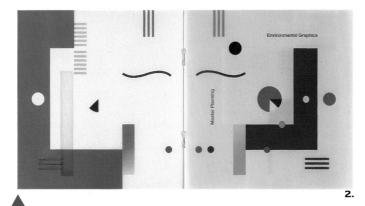

Cover (1), closed gatefold (2) and open gatefold (3) of 40th anniversary announcement.

DESIGN FIRM: Walter/ Johnsen, Los Angeles, California

DESIGNER: Steve Johnsen

ART DIRECTOR: Eileen Avery, Eileen Avery Design

1.

2.

3.

Chaix Johnson International
Retail interiors

GEORGE RICE & SONS

Electronic Prepress

2.

Cover (1) and spreads

(2,3) from capabilities

brochure for electronic

prepress system.

DESIGN FIRM: Robert

Miles Runyan &

Associates, Playa del

Ray, California

DESIGNER: Gary Hinsche

PHOTOGRAPHY: Robert

Stevens Photography

3.

1.

George Rice & Sons

Printing

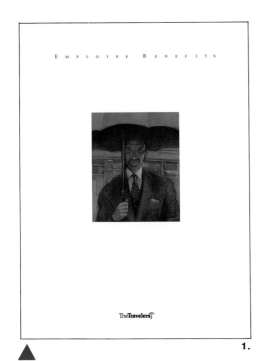

1.

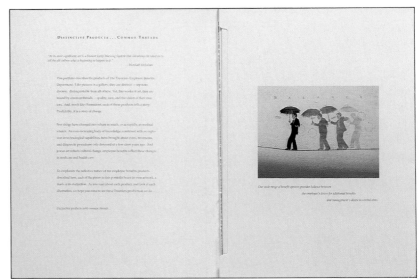

2.

3.

4.

Cover (1) and interior (2) of folder containing promotional brochures that explain the company's employee benefit plans; covers (6,7,8,9), spreads (3,4) and spot illustration (5) from brochures.

DESIGN FIRM: Pollard Design, East Hartland, Connecticut

ART DIRECTOR: Jeff Pollard

DESIGNERS: Jeff and Adrienne Pollard

ILLUSTRATORS: Gary Kelley, Jeff Pollard, Anthony Russo, Vivienne Flesher

5.   Insurance

The Travelers Insurance

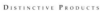

The Travelers

6.

The Travelers

7.

The Travelers

8.

The Travelers

9.

1.

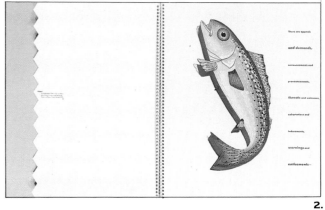

2.

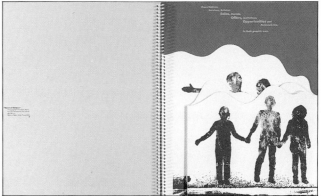

3.

4.

Simpson Paper

Paper products

Cover (1), spreads (2,3) and spot illustration (4) from promotional sales brochure.

DESIGN FIRM: Cross Associates, Los Angeles, California

ART DIRECTOR/ DESIGNER: John Clark

DESIGNER: Paul Langland

PHOTOGRAPHER: Jay Maisel

DON'T GIVE UP ON
HIGH SCHOOL, UNTIL
YOU'VE TRIED COLLEGE.

1.

Educational institution

Cover (1) and interior (2)

of foldout brochure for

high-school dropout

program.

ART DIRECTOR: Bill

Freeland/LaGuardia

Communications, Long

Island City, New York

DESIGNER/

ILLUSTRATOR:

Martin Carrichner

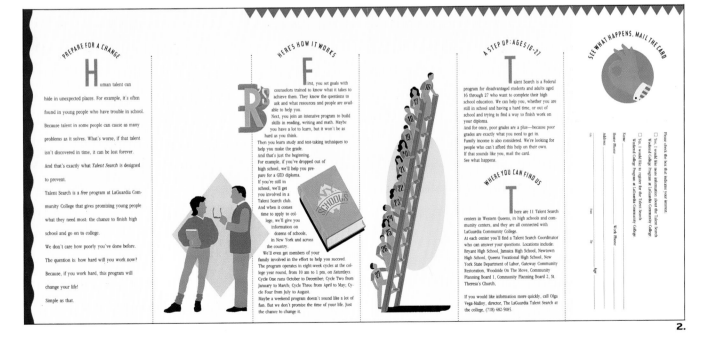

PREPARE FOR A CHANGE

Human talent can

hide in unexpected places. For example, it's often

found in young people who have trouble in school.

Because talent in some people can cause as many

problems as it solves. What's worse, if that talent

isn't discovered in time, it can be lost forever.

And that's exactly what *Talent Search* is designed

to prevent.

Talent Search is a *free* program at LaGuardia Com-

munity College that gives promising young people

what they need most: the chance to finish high

school and go on to college.

We don't care how poorly you've done before.

The question is: how hard will you work *now*?

Because, if you work hard, this program will

change your life!

Simple as that.

HERE'S HOW IT WORKS

First, you set goals with

counselors trained to know what it takes to

achieve them. They know the questions to

ask and what resources and people are avail-

able to help you.

Next, you join an intensive program to build

skills in reading, writing and math. Maybe

you have a lot to learn, but it won't be as

hard as you think.

Then you learn study and test-taking techniques to

help you make the grade.

And that's just the beginning.

For example, if you've dropped out of

high school, we'll help you pre-

pare for a GED diploma.

If you're still in

school, we'll get

you involved in a

Talent Search club.

And when it comes

time to apply to col-

lege, we'll give you

information on

dozens of schools,

in New York and across

the country.

We'll even get members of your

family involved in the effort to help you succeed.

The program operates in eight-week cycles at the col-

lege year round, from 10 am to 1 pm, on *Saturdays*.

Cycle One runs October to December; Cycle Two from

January to March; Cycle Three from April to May; Cy-

cle Four from July to August.

Maybe a weekend program doesn't sound like a lot of

fun. But we don't promise the time of your life. Just

the chance to change it.

A STEP UP: AGES 16-27

Talent Search is a Federal

program for disadvantaged students and adults aged

16 through 27 who want to complete their high

school education. We can help you, whether you are

still in school and having a hard time, or out of

school and trying to find a way to finish work on

your diploma.

And for once, poor grades are a plus—because poor

grades are exactly what you need to get in.

Family income is also considered. We're looking for

people who can't afford this help on their own.

If that sounds like you, mail the card.

See what happens.

WHERE YOU CAN FIND US

There are 11 Talent Search

centers in Western Queens, in high schools and com-

munity centers, and they are all connected with

LaGuardia Community College.

At each center you'll find a Talent Search Coordinator

who can answer your questions. Locations include:

Bryant High School, Jamaica High School, Newtown

High School, Queens Vocational High School, New

York State Department of Labor, Gateway Community

Restoration, Woodside On The Move, Community

Planning Board 1, Community Planning Board 2, St.

Theresa's Church.

If you would like information more quickly, call Olga

Vega-Malloy, director, The LaGuardia Talent Search at

the college, (718) 482-5085.

SEE WHAT HAPPENS, MAIL THE CARD

Please check the box that indicates your interest:

☐ Yes, I would like more information about the Talent Search

☐ Yes, I would like to register for the Talent Search
Weekend College Program at LaGuardia Community College.

☐ Yes, I would like to register for the Talent Search
Weekend College Program at LaGuardia Community College.

Name

Home Phone   Work Phone

Address

City   State   Zip   Age

2.

1.

2.

Cover (1) and spreads
(2,3) from fundraising
brochure directed at local
business community.

DESIGN FIRM:

Muller+Company,

Kansas City, Missouri

ART DIRECTOR:

John Muller

DESIGNER: Jane Weeks

PRODUCTION ARTIST:

James Dettner

COPYWRITER:

John Kreuger

PHOTOGRAPHERS:

Mike Regnier, Gary

Sutton

3.

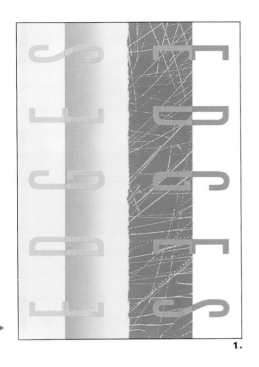

1.

2.

3.

Cover (1), spreads (2,3)

and spot illustration (4)

from promotional

brochure.

DESIGN FIRM:

Muller + Company,

Kansas City, Missouri

ART DIRECTOR/

DESIGNER: John Muller

DESIGNER: Jane Weeks

PRODUCTION ART:

James Dettner

COPYWRITER:

David Marks

PHOTOGRAPHER:

Michael Regnier

4.

Strathmore Paper

Paper products

Food products

1.

2.

3.

5.

4.

Cover (1), cover insert (2) and spread (3) from first in a series of brochures promoting customer service programs and policies; second brochure in series, shown in paper bag sleeve (4); cover insert (5) and spread (6) from second brochure.

DESIGN FIRM: Katz Wheeler Design, Philadelphia, Pennsylvania

ART DIRECTOR: Joseph Perrone, Lewis Gilman & Kynett

6.

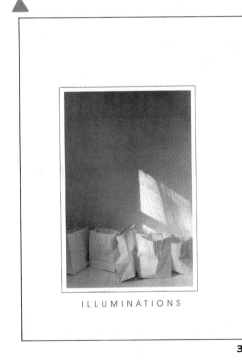

Blues on Astrolite.

1.

2.

ILLUMINATIONS

3.

4.

Monadnock Paper Mills

Paper products

Cover (1) and spread (2) from promotional series for Astrolite; cover (3) and spread (4) from additional brochure in series.

DESIGN FIRM: Rob MacIntosh Communications, Boston, Massachusetts

DESIGNER: Rob MacIntosh

ILLUSTRATOR: Vivienne Flesher

CALLIGRAPHER: Jean Evans

PHOTOGRAPHER: Lilo Raymond

Office interiors

1.

Cover (1) and spreads
(2,3) from booklet
announcing, and inviting
participation in, a new
communication process
implemented at the
company's Corporate
Design Center.

DESIGN FIRM: Fitch
RichardsonSmith,
Worthington, Ohio

ART DIRECTORS:
Jaimie Alexander, Shelly
Evenson, John
Rheinfrank, Austin
Henderson

DESIGNER: Kwok C.
(Peter) Chan

WRITER: Wendie Wulff

ILLUSTRATOR:
Malcolm Tarlofsky

PHOTOGRAPHER:
Steven Trank

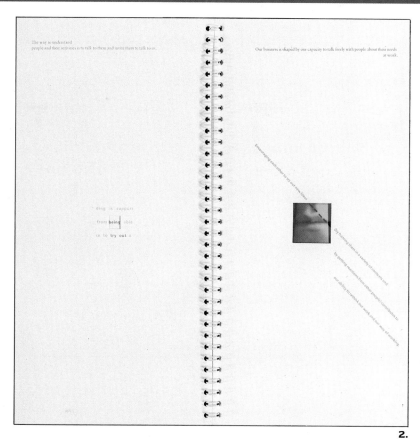

2.

3.

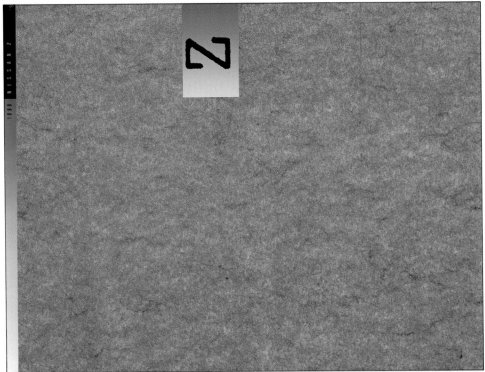

1.

2.

Cover (2), spot illustrations (3) and spreads (4,5) from promotional consumer brochure for 300 ZX; sleeve (1).

DESIGN FIRM: The Designory, Inc., Long Beach, California

CREATIVE DIRECTOR: David Almquist

CREATIVE/ART DIRECTOR/DESIGNER: Lynne Grigg

DESIGNERS: Paul Ison, Lisa Langhoff

PHOTOGRAPHER: Bob Grigg (2)

3.

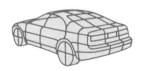

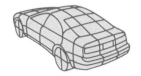

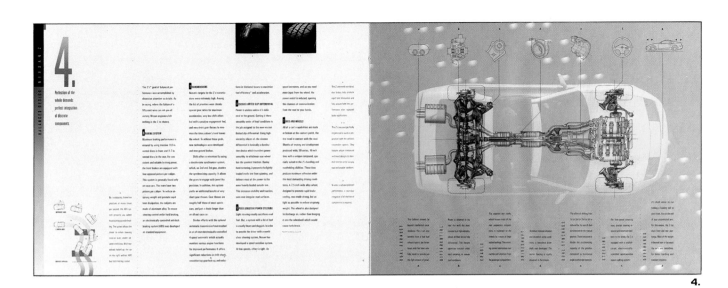

4.

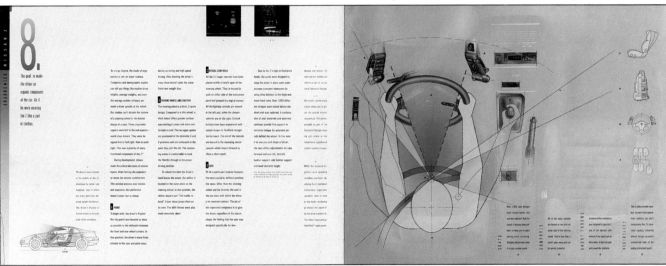

5.

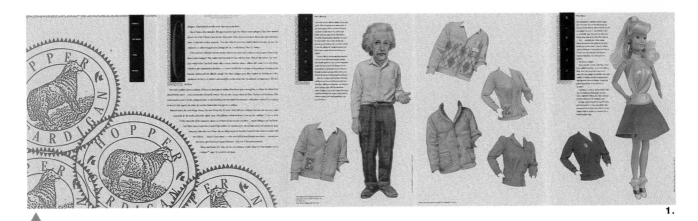

1.

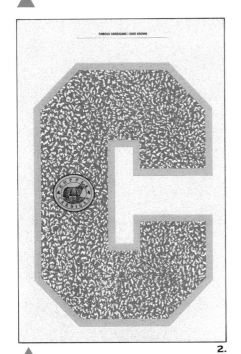

2.

3.

4.

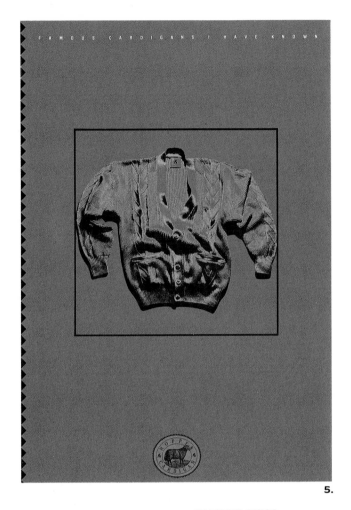

FAMOUS CARDIGANS I HAVE KNOWN

5.

6.

Four-part direct mail campaign promoting Cardigan paper. Shown are inside spread from a foldout brochure (1); cover (2), first spread (3) and final spread (4) from a foldout piece; cover of a brochure (5); cover of a foldout piece (6); envelope (7).

DESIGN FIRM:
HarrisonSimmons, Inc.,
Dallas, Texas
ART DIRECTOR:
Arthur Simmons
ART DIRECTOR/
DESIGNER/
ILLUSTRATOR:
Richard Gavos
PHOTOGRAPHER:
Richard Reens
ILLUSTRATORS: Rick
Kronniger, Chris F.
Payne, Melissa Grimes

7.

1.

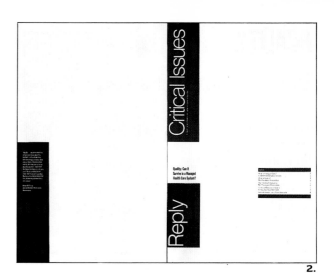

2.

3.

Lutheran General Hospital

Health care

Cover (1) and spreads (2,3) from tabloid-size publication directed at community business leaders.

DESIGN FIRM: Kym Abrams Design, Chicago, Illinois

ART DIRECTOR:

Kym Abrams

DESIGNER:

Sandi Weindling

PHOTOGRAPHER:

Eric Hausman

ILLUSTRATOR: Quang Ho

WRITER: Giudi Weiss

1.

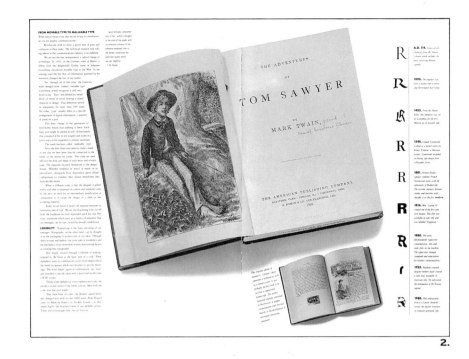

2.

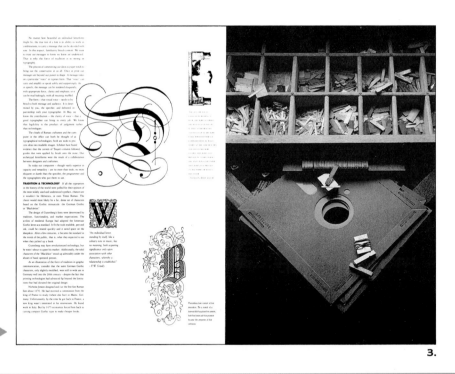

3.

Cover (1) and spreads
(2,3) from premiere issue
of a promotional
magazine directed at
local designers, art
directors and other type
specifiers.
DESIGN FIRM: The
Kuester Group, Inc.,
Minneapolis, Minnesota

May Type

Typesetting

CREATIVE DIRECTOR:

David Forney

ART DIRECTOR/

DESIGNER: Bob Goebel

1.

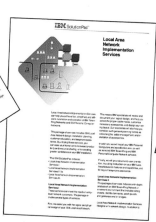

2.

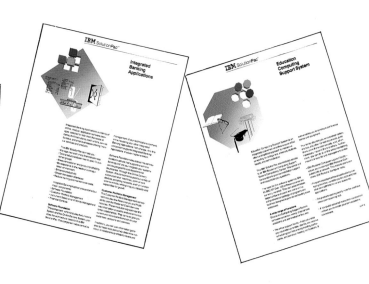

3.

4.

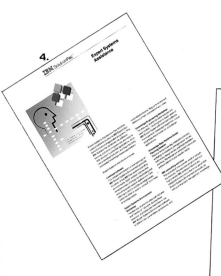

IBM

Computer hardware and software

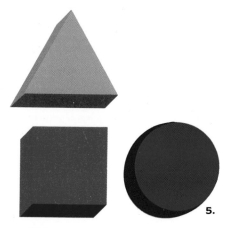

5.

Folder covers (1,2,3) and information sheets (4) from series of brochures promoting IBM Solution Pacs (hardware/software combinations for specific industry applications); spot illustration (5) from series.

DESIGN FIRM: Jones, Medinger, Kindschi, Bushko, North Salem, New York

ART DIRECTOR/ DESIGNER/ ILLUSTRATOR: Don Kindschi

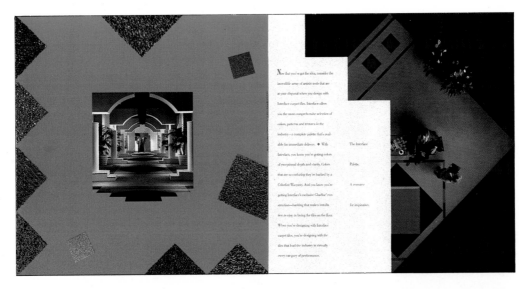

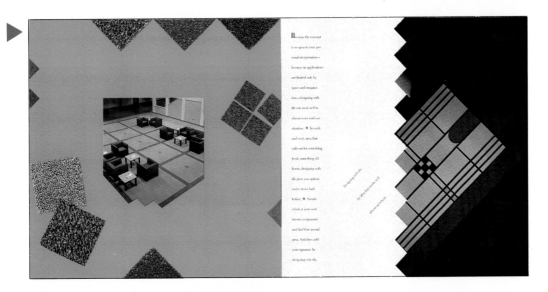

Spreads from promotional brochure directed at interior design market.

DESIGN FIRM: Wages Design, Atlanta, Georgia

DESIGNERS: Robert Wages, Karen Webster

PHOTOGRAPHER: Jonathan Hillyer

Interface Flooring

Interior flooring

Cover and interior of folder (1), spot illustrations (3) and direct-mail poster (2) for program directed at resellers that provides training and education for end users.
DESIGN FIRM: Collins Design Group, Inc., Lexington, Massachusetts

1.

DESIGNER/

ILLUSTRATOR:

Brian Collins

ILLUSTRATOR:

Rob Cline

COPYWRITER:

Christine Kane

TYPOGRAPHER:

Wordtech

PRINTING: Pride Printers

2.

Digital Equipment
Computer hardware and software

3.

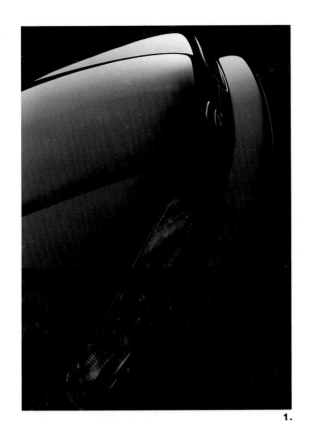

1.

2.

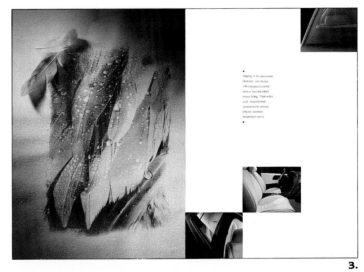

3.

Nissan Motor/Infiniti Division

Automotive

Cover (1) and spreads (2,3) from brochure introducing the Infiniti. DESIGN FIRM: Hill, Holliday, Boston, Massachusetts

ART DIRECTOR/ DESIGNER: Vic Cevoli

DESIGNER: John Avery

PHOTOGRAPHER: Clint Clemens

COPYWRITER: Neill Ray

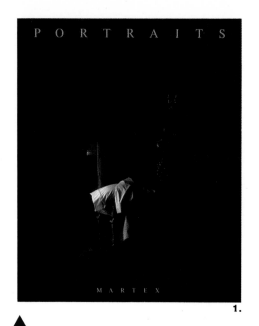

1.

2.

3.

WestPoint Pepperell

Home furnishings

Cover (1) and spreads (2,3) from promotional sales brochure directed at distributors.

DESIGN FIRM:

Designframe, Inc., New York, New York

ART DIRECTOR/ DESIGNER:

James Sebastian

DESIGNER:

Junko Mayumi

INTERIOR DESIGNER:

William Walter

PHOTOGRAPHER:

Bruce Wolf

76

THIS IS MIMER.
The ancient Norse gods came
to him for access to the well
of knowledge.
A thousand years later,
data processing managers are
learning to do the same.

1.

In Switzerland, there is a shortage of experienced computer programmers. So Jürg Roos knew it was more than just a database he would need for the industrial plant division of ASEA Brown-Boveri Switzerland. He'd need tools that would help him to create and maintain applications with ease.

That's why he came to Mimer.

MIMER/PG is Mimer's fourth-generation language tool. Unlike other 4GL tools, MIMER/PG generates *actual 3GL code*. You choose the best language for the application at hand — "C", FORTRAN or COBOL. MIMER/PG does the rest, using your 4GL commands to write the programme. Since the generated programme is optimised 3GL code, you can add your own 3GL routines in the traditional way.

MIMER/PG has cut development time by half and even more for some users. And because Mimer applications are portable, they can be developed economically in one computer environment and then run in another.

Once the programme is complete, maintenance with MIMER/PG is simple — it can start right at the prototype level. It's not unusual to reduce maintenance time by 80 percent or more.

MIMER/PG is only the beginning. Mimer has a range of development tools designed to simplify all aspects of programming.

MIMER/SQL is a structured query language that can be used for development and ad hoc retrievals. It supports referential integrity — something long overdue in relational databases.

MIMER/FM is a screen forms manager that works in both synchronous and asynchronous environments. MIMER/RG — Report Generator — is an easy-to-use tool for defining, storing, updating and running output formats on screen or paper.

Mimer run-time tools make it easy for end-users to get the most out of a system, even if they have no computer experience. MIMER/SQL — the run-time version — lets them find information with simple commands. MIMER/QF — query by forms — helps users enter, update and delete data as well as retrieve it. The end-user version of MIMER/RG lets them design their own reports.

With these development and end-user tools, it's possible to improve the productivity of those who design and use Mimer. Which can't help but improve the overall performance of the system itself.

JÜRG ROOS needed to develop
applications with little effort.
And maintain them with virtually
no effort at all.

2.

3.

The great tree Yggdrasil, the ancients believed, held up the world. At its foot lay the well of knowledge — source of all information and wisdom. And guarding it stood the wise Mimer.

Mimer, you might say, was the founder of information management.

The modern Mimer — MIMER/DB — became a commercial product in 1980, after seven years of development and refinement. Today it is the leading RDBMS in Sweden and is well established in 18 other countries.

One reason for this success is that the products are only part of what we at Mimer Software have to offer.

First, our staff of consultants can help you before and during application development. We'll analyse your company and your needs to help you determine what kind of system is necessary. Or even if you need a new system at all. (More than once we have saved a customer from enormous expense by recommending a change in business procedures instead of a costly new computer system.)

You can use our consultants for project management, to reinforce your own development staff or to develop and implement turnkey projects.

In addition to our own staff, there are more than 100 Mimer-knowledgeable consultants in independent companies.

Mimer offers extensive training, with scheduled courses in our offices, or special sessions in yours. In addition to these, we also offer courses on important general topics, such as relational database design.

Finally, Mimer assures you of continuous support. We have an international support staff of 30 at headquarters in Uppsala, Sweden. As well as the dedicated staff of our agents and subsidiaries throughout Europe.

Find out more about how Mimer can give you the performance and flexibility you have been looking for in a relational database to provide.

Meet the missionaries of Nordic
mythology.

4.

Mimer Software

Computer software

Cover (1), spreads (2,4) and illustration (3) from promotional brochure.

DESIGN FIRM: Anderson & Lembke, Stamford, Connecticut

ART DIRECTOR:

Jeff Pappalardo

ILLUSTRATOR:

Frank Riccio

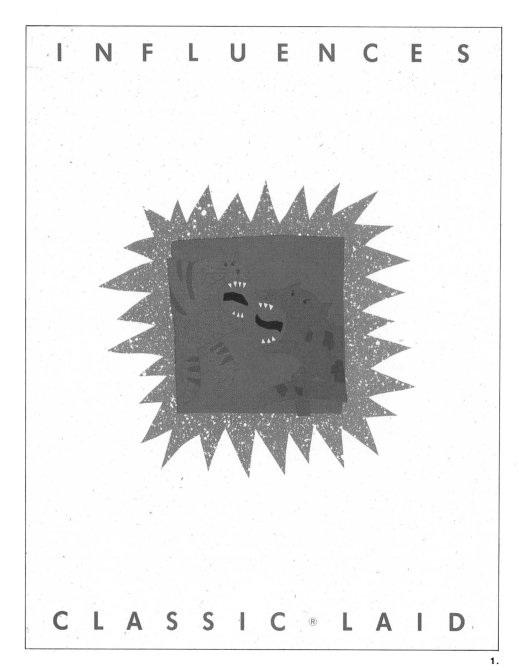

I N F L U E N C E S

C L A S S I C ® L A I D

1.

Promotional brochure. Shown are cover (1), spot illustration (2), spread (3), spread with closed gatefold (4), and same spread with open gatefold (5).

DESIGN FIRM: Sullivan Perkins, Dallas, Texas

DESIGNER/ ILLUSTRATOR: Ron Sullivan

ILLUSTRATORS: Jon Flaming, Linda Helton, Clark Richardson, Michael Sprong

COPYWRITER: Mark Perkins

2.

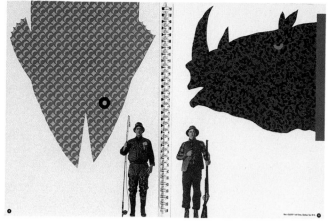

3.

4.

5.

Travelers Insurance

Insurance

Travel Agency Insurance Program

TheTravelers

Pizza Shop Owners Insurance Program

TheTravelers

Booksellers Insurance Program

TheTravelers

Professional Pet Groomers Insurance Program

TheTravelers

Pharmacists Insurance Program

TheTravelers

Chinese Restaurant Insurance Program

TheTravelers

Covers of a series of brochures directed at various small businesses.

ART DIRECTOR:

Kathleen Damiata/The Travelers Corporate Communications, Hartford, Connecticut

CREATIVE DIRECTOR:

Dallas Powell

DESIGNERS: Kathleen Damiata, Ginny McCullough

PHOTOGRAPHER:

Jeffrey Yardis

COPYWRITERS:

Linda Carpino, Andrea Vecchiolla

2.

1.

PARTNERS IN GROWTH

ART DIRECTOR/

DESIGNER: Ed Foster

DESIGNERS: Suzy
McCarthy, Cynthia Foster

ILLUSTRATOR:

Guy Billout

3i

Venture capital

Covers (1,4) and spreads
(2,3) from capabilities
brochures focusing on
specific venture capital
areas.

DESIGN FIRM: Foster
Design Group, Boston,
Massachusetts

3.

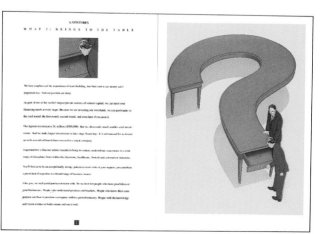

BUILDING BUSINESSES WORLDWIDE

4.

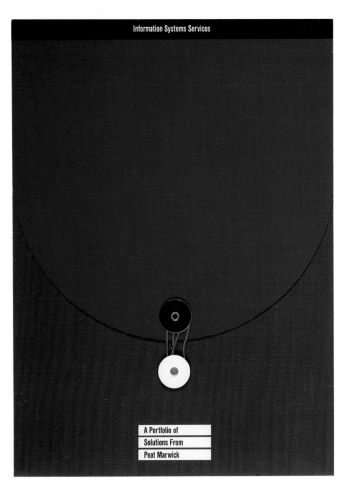

Information Systems Services

A Portfolio of
Solutions From
Peat Marwick

1.

KPMG Peat Marwick

Maryland State
Universities and Colleges
Get High Marks for
Distributed System
Implementation

2.

Peat Marwick

Information systems services

4.

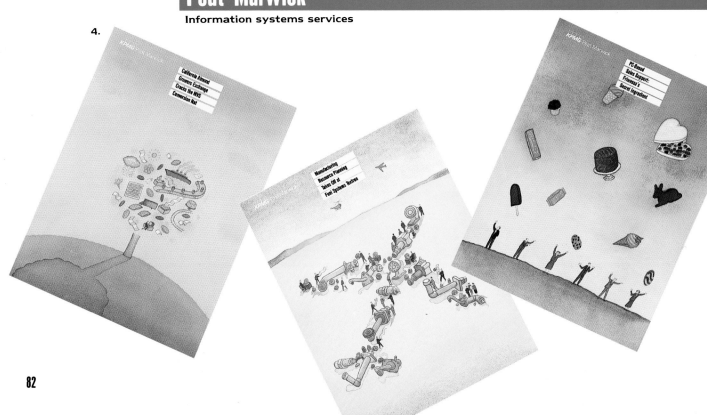

KPMG Peat Marwick

California Almond
Growers Exchange
Cracks the NVS
Conversion Nut

Manufacturing
Resource Planning
Takes Off at
Fuel Systems Textron

KPMG Peat Marwick

PC-Based
Sales Support:
Frieroza's
Secret Ingredient

Replacing its old student information and personnel systems with integrated on-line software threatened to be a trial by fire for Maryland State Universities and Colleges. But with Peat Marwick's help, they passed the test with flying colors, meeting all of their objectives and gaining important organizational growth in the process.

How do you get users from eight different organizations to implement two major information systems in a distributed processing environment—in less than two years? Effective project management is the key, as the experience of the Maryland State Universities and Colleges (MSUC) has shown. With an assist from Peat Marwick, MSUC turned the challenge of large-scale change into an opportunity for organizational growth.

Through generous support of its state universities and colleges, the Maryland legislature enriches the lives of its citizens and strengthens the foundation of its economic future. To provide the broadest possible educational opportunities for the people of Maryland, the Board of Trustees of the State Universities and Colleges operates six institutions of higher learning, dispersed across the state—from the historic Eastern Shore of Chesapeake Bay, through Maryland's urban centers, and westward to the Appalachian Mountains.

A Distributed Approach

Successfully managing so diverse and far-flung an enterprise means striking a fine balance between the Trustees' need to maintain statewide administrative and educational standards and the responsibility of each institution to effectively address the special needs of the community it serves.

Central to MSUC's strategy for maintaining this balance is a unique distributed approach to data processing. Established by the 1980 Consolidated Administrative and Academic Data Processing Plan, "coordinated network processing" gives each institution the autonomy and flexibility of operating its own computers, while ensuring system-wide coordination through the leadership of the Management Information Network Center—MINC, for short.

As the Board's data processing arm, MINC is responsible for implementing the 1980 plan, and for managing a network of 28 Digital Equipment Company VAX minicomputers dispersed throughout the MSUC system's six institutions, at two schools

> The process itself... has firmly established the orientation and channels of communication necessary to make coordinated network processing a reality at MSUC.

governed by separate Boards, and at MINC.

MINC's role is pivotal. By centralizing expensive technical resources, and consolidating purchasing power, MINC reduces the cost of giving each institution its own data processing operation. And by coordinating the acquisition, maintenance, and support of hardware and software used throughout the entire system, MINC guarantees the Board ready access to the complete, consistent, and compatible data it needs to provide state-wide leadership.

A Test of Their Faith

During the plan's early years, MINC Director Gregory Petz and his staff effectively led MSUC's transition to the distributed hardware environment. They also established the framework for all administrative processing by installing Information Associates' state-of-the-art Financial Records System, and selecting the same vendor's Student Information System (SIS) and Human Resource System (HRS) to replace ancient, inadequate software.

Now, however, MSUC's commitment to coordinated network processing faced its toughest test. For the fate of the 1980 plan hinged on MINC's ability to manage the pervasive changes in organizational structure and culture entailed by implementation of SIS and HRS.

High-level direction of the effort was provided by Michael Langrehr, the Board's Associate Executive Director for Finance. Langrehr knew full well what he was up against: "Replacing critical systems is never easy," he notes. "You have to take a hard look at time-honored policies, redefine responsibilities, and, in some cases, redraw functional lines. It all adds up to an immense strain—for any organization."

For MSUC, however, the challenge was especially complex. Coordinated network processing called for running the same administrative software throughout the network. "To put in systems that satisfied all eight schools," explains Langrehr, "we had to develop sustained, widespread cooperation among institutions, departments, and individuals—something we had not done as well as we would have liked in the past, particularly in the area of data processing."

Organizing for Consensus

There was really only one acceptable solution. "Since the colleges and universities are the primary users," Langrehr explains, "we had to get all eight of them deeply involved in this project right from the beginning." That, as Langrehr well knew, was easier said than done. Working at the most detailed level, key users from every functional area in every school had to reach consensus on precisely how the packages would be modified and installed. "After all," explained Langrehr, "if they weren't completely satisfied, MINC would suffer the consequences."

For the project management expertise necessary to orchestrate a broad-based, aggressive implementation effort, MSUC turned to Peat Marwick. "With the amount of resources we had committed, and the risks involved," explains Langrehr, "we needed people who had been through this before; people with the technical and management skills to keep all of our horses pulling in the same direction."

Peat Marwick began by helping MINC Director Petz establish an effective project structure. At its head was a Steering Committee chaired by Mike Langrehr and composed of senior Board staff, key users from the various institutions, as well as representatives from Peat Marwick and the software vendor, Information Associates.

The Steering Committee provided general direction for the six "application teams"—one for each major subsystem—which were the project's basic working units. Each application team included users from the relevant

> For MSUC as a whole, the project's success demonstrates the ability of coordinated efforts to meet the diverse needs of all eight institutions.

functional area at every institution, plus MINC and Board staff, a Peat Marwick project manager, and an Information Associates software specialist.

Clearing the Air

Not surprisingly, setting up the project structure and direction soon brought to the fore fundamental concerns regarding the coordinated network strategy. In particular, the Data Processing Coordinators of all eight institutions felt that MINC's role needed rethinking. In a letter to Langrehr, they questioned the wisdom of centralizing so much control over software development in a single office reporting directly to the Board. The needs of the various institutions, they thought, would be better served by placing MINC under a system-wide committee, and giving each school more direct control over software maintenance.

The seriousness and impact of these concerns was evident to Langrehr. "We had to address these issues quickly and decisively," he explains.

"If we did not get the institutions fully on board, the project was in trouble—and with it, the whole concept of a coordinated network."

Langrehr therefore asked Peat Marwick to review the Data Processing Coordinators' proposal, and recommend alternatives for resolving the key issues.

Based on a thorough analysis of the proposal in light of the 1980 plan and subsequent developments, the consulting team recommended that MSUC reaffirm the original strategy, which had been adopted previously. Peat Marwick also detailed a series of steps to address the Data Processing Coordinators' specific concerns within the framework of the original plan. These recommendations were soon approved both by the Council of Presidents and by the Board of Trustees.

Moving Forward

Having confronted the major underlying issues, the project team could focus its full energy on system implementation. For the application teams, this meant meeting regularly to identify "issues"—mismatches between the new system and existing administrative procedures and needs. After considering an issue's varying impact on the eight schools involved, the team recommended either modifying the software to accommodate current procedures, or changing policies or procedures to accommodate the software.

These recommendations went to high-level Review and Analysis Teams—one for each major system. Each "RA team" included a member of the Board Staff coordinating user efforts, a MINC data processing analyst, a Peat Marwick project manager, and a representative from the software vendor. With their broader system perspective and data processing expertise, the RA teams worked to ensure efficiency and consistency across applications in the resolution of all issues.

Although complex and somewhat bureaucratic, this structure provided an ideal framework for resolving the inevitable technical and territorial disputes inherent in a project of this size and scope, while maintaining forward momentum. It was also efficient, allowing application teams—working in parallel—to resolve literally hundreds of issues on their own in a relatively short time. This in turn enabled senior project managers to focus on large-scale coordination and those few user concerns that could not be resolved at lower levels.

3.

Covers (2,4) and spread (3) from series of brochures presenting case histories of clients; pouch (1) containing the brochures.

DESIGN FIRM:

Pentagram Design, New York, New York

ART DIRECTOR:

Peter Harrison

DESIGNER:

Susan Hochbaum

ILLUSTRATOR:

Lonni Sue Johnson

1.

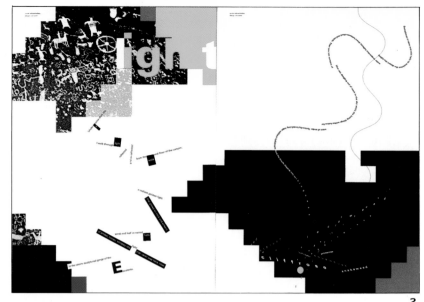

2.

3.

Educational institution

Cover (1) and spreads (2,3) from "Typography: Medium & Message" symposium brochure (also used as capabilities brochure by sponsor of symposium,

LinoTypographers/ Lithographers).

DESIGN FIRM: Meggs & Meggs, Richmond, Virginia

ART DIRECTOR: Margie Adkins

DESIGNERS: Philip B. Meggs, Rob Carter, Betty Bins, Rudy Vanderlans, Margie Adkins

TYPESETTER/PRINTER: LinoTypographics/ Lithographers

1.

2.

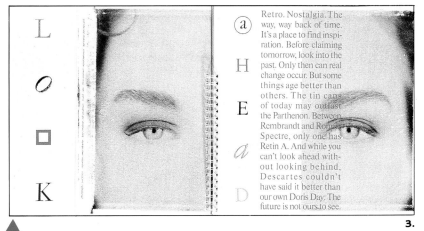

3.

Cover (1), spreads (2,3,4)
and spot symbol (5) for
image and fundraising
brochure.

DESIGN FIRM:

Frankenberry, Laughlin &
Constable, Milwaukee,
Wisconsin

ART DIRECTOR:

Mark Koerner

PHOTOGRAPHER:

Joseph Picayo

PHOTO ASSISTANT:

Darryl Patterson

4.

5.

Milwaukee Institute of Art & Design

Educational institution

What we receive: MDE forms, the IOF, and calls for help.

The SingleFile Form collects the federally-required information needed to determine eligibility for federal Title IV student aid programs, including the Stafford Loan Program.

Then the form asks four other questions to help FAOs process the student's financial aid and assemble the award package: planned enrollment status, planned enrollment period, housing plans, and number of prior schools attended.

The Institutional Options Form (IOF) makes it simple to tell us the level of service you want from us. You'll need to fill it out before we can process need analysis for your school. On this form you'll specify what kinds of output you want, to customize the service to your financial aid system. You'll have a choice of receiving information via tape, paper, or electronic transmission to your mainframe or to your PC using WhizKid software.

Free assistance is available to you and your students. Questions will be answered fast by people who actually know what they're talking about. Students can dial a toll-free assistance number. For schools, a special need analysis staff will answer MDE questions, and a special electronic services staff will answer data transmission questions.

20 questions to the SingleFile Form, vs. more than 100 questions on certain other MDE forms: the not enough question on the federal guarantor's form. The SingleFile Form is complex, clear, and less work to fill out.

1.

The EDE network can simplify your work if you state a preference for the SingleFile Form.

How? Consistency. Because through the EDE (Electronic Data Exchange) network you'll get all of your student records in one standard format—a format you choose—regardless of the source.

A student can use the SingleFile Form, or forms from CSS, ACT, the federal government, or whomever. Yet your office receives the information in whatever format you want.

You don't have to redesign your computer system.

You don't have to accept multiple MDE formats.

You don't have to pay for as many computer tapes, or as many electronic transmissions, or as many manhours of data entry.

You don't have to force freshmen applying to several schools to fill out more than one MDE application. You can remain "form neutral" with the EDE network in place.

It saves you time. It saves students time.

And when you combine the EDE network with the MDE-meets-loan connection, you can receive an automatic loan application *no matter which MDE form the student submits.*

And becoming part of the EDE network takes nothing but a preference for USA Funds' SingleFile Form.

Assume you've gone. Let's say 8 hours is an average workday. The less of that four you spend on paperwork, the more you can spend on real work, like counseling, running and finding grants and scholarships for students.

2.

United Student Aid Funds
Financial aid for education

Spreads (1,2) and spot illustration (3) from capabilities brochure directed at financial aid officers at educational institutions.

DESIGN FIRM: Young & Laramore, Indianapolis, Indiana

DESIGNER: Chris Beatty

PHOTOGRAPHER: Darlene Delbecq

COPYWRITER: Charlie Hopper

3.

1.

2.

3.

Cover (1), spreads (2,3) and spot illustration (4) from recruitment catalog for people exploring new careers in design.

DESIGN FIRM:

Clifford Selbert Design,

Cambridge,

Massachusetts

ART DIRECTOR:

Clifford Selbert

DESIGNER: Jean Wilcox

ILLUSTRATOR:

David Linn

4.

Harvard University Graduate School of Design

Educational institution

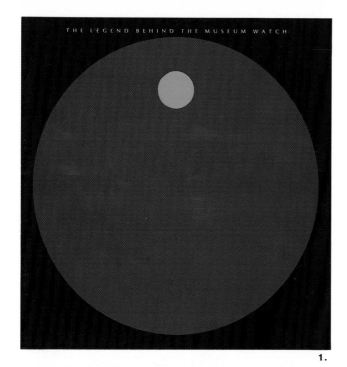

1.

Movado Watch

Timepieces

Cover (1) and spreads (2,3) from brochure announcing the "Museum Design" product launch; cover (4) and spread (5) from one of a series of collateral pieces in the same launch.

DESIGN FIRM: The Design Office, Inc., New York, New York

CREATIVE DIRECTOR: Charles Davidson

DESIGNER: Joseph Feigenbaum

PHOTOGRAPHER: John Manno

COPYWRITER: Deanne Dunning

ILLUSTRATOR: Michael Koester

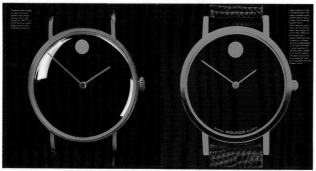

2.

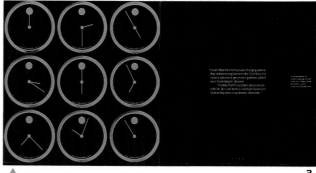

3.

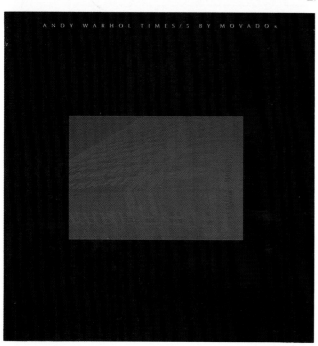

4.

5.

Phil's Photo/Harold's Hues

Photolettering/Art studio

Covers of rates and
services brochures.
DESIGNER: James
Hellmuth, Takoma Park,
Maryland
ILLUSTRATOR: Ed Musey

1. The business world. Blue suit. Striped tie. And the knowledge to succeed. As a student in our business administration curriculum, you'll learn about all areas of business. You can choose to specialize in accounting, economics, finance, general business, management, management information systems or marketing. Many students who've graduated from our accounting program have become CPAs. Finance majors have become bankers and stockbrokers. Some of our graduates have started their own businesses. Whatever your interest, whether it be in management, marketing, or computers, our degree program in business administration can open a lot of doors. 2. How to get two steps ahead of the competition. Qualified students get the opportunity in our internship program to work for area corporations and receive full academic credit. Many students have found this to be a great chance to line up a job for after graduation. Speaking of life after graduation, our Career Development and Placement Service is very active in helping graduates start their careers. Each year, over 75 corporations interview on campus. Major corporations to mid-sized to smaller regional companies. 3. Public administration. The workings of government. Our program in public administration will help you gain an insight into the American political system. How government policy is created, implemented and, in turn, how that policy affects everyone in society. The subject matter can be fascinating and very useful for those interested in careers in business, politics and law. (You could also end up spending a semester in our nation's capital through our Washington Internship Program.) 4. For those who want to delve further back into history than "The Life and Times of John, Paul, George and Ringo," our history major is an option. Or maybe you'd rather *visit* the land of John, Paul, George and Ringo. You can spend a semester overseas studying the history and culture of England in cooperation with Regent's College, London. 5. What's going on inside that brain of yours? Why do people behave the way they do? These are just some of the questions you'll study as a psychology major. Another degree option is our program in social service which combines the disciplines of psychology, sociology, and public administration to prepare you for a career in human services, the caring profession.

Spreads from college recruitment brochure.

DESIGN FIRM:

Noble + Wecal, Boston, Massachusetts

ART DIRECTOR:

Dean Noble

PHOTOGRAPHER:

John Curtis

COPYWRITER:

David Wecal

HAND COLORING:

John Curtis, Pamela Strauss

1. One of the nice things about Nichols is when you sit down in the school snackbar the person behind the counter already knows how you like your eggs and how many sugars you take in your coffee. Try getting service like that in a big school. 2. Rita Gatzke and Jean Healey have been moms to thousands of Nichols students. Rita says, "I feel like I'm full-time manager and part-time psychiatrist." Students have a problem, Rita and Jean are always there to listen. 3. Here at Nichols we have something called the Nickie Chickie. Students say it's the most incredibly-unbelievably-outrageous sandwich you can get in Dudley, Massachusetts for $1.75. The folks in the cafeteria say you can't graduate without trying one. 4. A few important facts about the food at Nichols. Our food service provides three nutritionally balanced meals a day, Monday through Friday. Two meals, Saturday and Sunday. (Your parents will be relieved to hear that.) The meals at Nichols are actually quite good. (*You'll* be relieved to hear that.) 5. Rumor has it that munching on the world famous Nickie Burger while studying calculus can make all those formulas seem a little less complicated. Who are we to argue?

Nichols College

Educational institution

Home furnishings

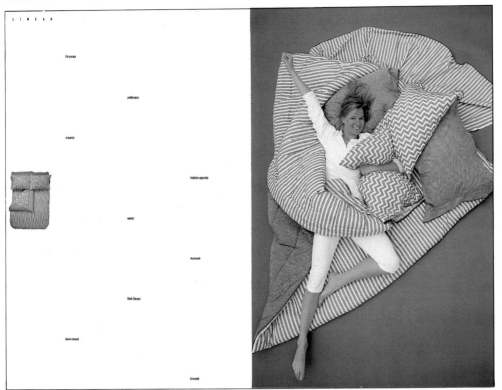

1.

2.

Cover (2) and spreads (1,3) from bed and bath furnishings promotional brochure.

DESIGN FIRM:

Vanderbyl Design, San Francisco, California

DESIGNER:

Michael Vanderbyl

PHOTOGRAPHERS:

Robert Carra, Sharon Risedorph

3.

CROWN BRITE BASICS

1.

2.

Cover (1), spread (2) and illustration (4) from promotional brochure; spread (3) from promotional folder in the same campaign.

3.

DESIGN FIRM: Cook and Shanosky Associates, Princeton, New Jersey

DESIGNERS: Roger Cook, Dan Shanosky

PHOTOGRAPHER: Paul Kopelow

COPYWRITERS: J. William Kelley (1,2,4), David L. Eynon (3)

4.

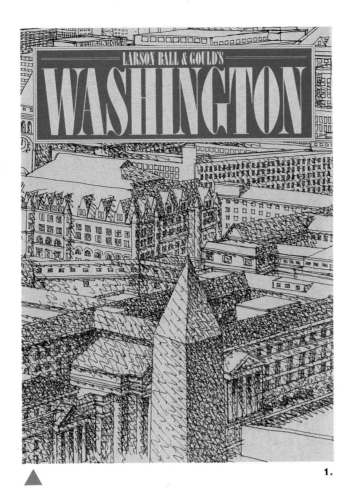

1.

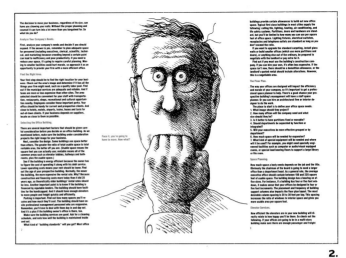

2.

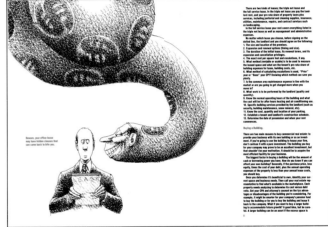

3.

Larson, Ball, & Gould

Commercial real estate

Cover (1), spreads (2,3) and illustration (4) from promotional brochure providing general information on the industry.

DESIGN MANAGEMENT:

The Brown Corporation, Baltimore, Maryland

DESIGNER:

Lyle Metzdorf, New York, New York

ILLUSTRATOR:

Fred Hilliard

4.

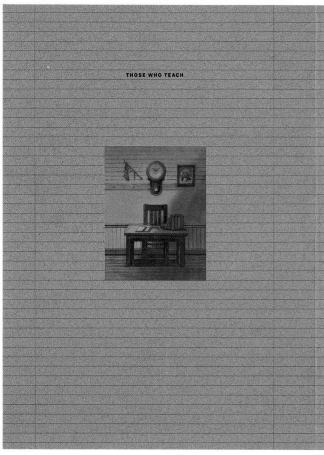

THOSE WHO TEACH

Simpson Paper
Paper products

Cover (1), spread (2) and

initial cap (3) from

promotional brochure

spotlighting the

American teacher.

DESIGN FIRM: Milton

Glaser, Inc., New York,

New York

DESIGNER: Milton Glaser

1.

MS. NAGATA

LORNA NAGATA
Fourth Grade Teacher, Fremont Elementary
Alhambra, California

Fremont Elementary, in the Los Angeles area near Pasadena, is half Hispanic and one quarter Asian. Lorna Nagata teaches all subjects to classes that number as many as thirty-eight children.

One way she teaches is through literature.

"We read whole works of literature. Or I read them stories, pieces of literature, poems, and we try to relate them to themselves and they seem to get a great deal of enjoyment from that."

Every spring, Ms. Nagata turns her class into a publishing company. The students write and illustrate picture books which are bound and donated to the school library.

"They're free to write about any area they feel comfortable with. What I want for them is the sense that they have the ability and the confidence to do whatever it is they want to do."

A native of Hawaii, Lorna Nagata wanted to be a teacher when she was in kindergarten, and has always wanted to be one.

"As a child, there were a couple of times I thought about nursing, and I went through that stage of wanting to be a veterinarian. But it was short-lived."

Lorna Nagata has been a teacher for sixteen years. Her husband is an elementary school Assistant Principal. They have two young sons, one in first grade and the other in third.

MR. MEIER

RICHARD MEIER
First Grade Teacher, John F. Kennedy Elementary
Sioux Falls, South Dakota

The first day of school for Richard Meier's class opens when he meets them outside on the playground.

"And then when I bring them into the room, they are so overwhelmed by a first grade classroom, you know. We sit down and start talking about how a classroom should be run and how the students can help, where the offices are, where the restrooms are."

Mr. Meier teaches all subjects. But it is when his students start learning to write stories that school comes alive for the teacher and his class.

The children begin by writing sentences and making a dictionary. As their abilities develop, they write short stories. By the end of the year they have written and illustrated their own books.

"I have never had a student who couldn't come up with a story. I have some who have written stories thirty to thirty-five pages. Others write very, very short stories. But I take everybody at their level and let them go. And they have all succeeded."

A six-footer, Richard Meier is constantly stooping and bending down with his first grade students. When he works with reading groups, he folds himself onto a child-size chair at a child-size table.

"When they start school, they might know a few words and can read basic sentences, but to watch the growth by spring, it is just fantastic."

Like teachers at all levels of education, Richard Meier says that the one thing he most wants his students to learn is self-esteem.

"There are a lot of children that come in and say, 'I can't do it. I can't read. Why even try?' They've been programmed even at that age with that kind of attitude. So that is one thing I really work on. I show them, hey, I can accomplish something."

Richard Meier attended Concordia College in Moorhead, Minnesota, and got his M.A. at the University of South Dakota. He and his wife have two daughters who attend the school where he teaches.

FLOSSIE

FLORENCE LEWIS
English Teacher, Lowell High School
San Francisco

Florence Lewis has long been known as Flossie to students, teachers, parents—and the local press. After teaching English for thirty-seven years, she recently raised holy hell to avert forced retirement. It was a long-running news story with a happy ending that delighted what appeared to be a substantial majority of San Franciscans.

Flossie has now returned to Berkeley for a Ph.D. while continuing to teach high school.

"A teacher has to go back to school. One has to keep it up. Teaching is always in part a power trip. Anyone who doesn't know that it is a power trip doesn't understand some of the job of teaching but also some of the agony. It is the use of power that is the constant challenge. How you use power, how not to use it, how not to abuse it.

"For me the real test is that you go and learn from people who are better than you are in several ways, that is to say, they have more knowledge, and they have more power, and you test your knowledge against theirs and your understanding of power against their use of power. If we had the ideal society, education wouldn't stop once you became a teacher. It has to continue."

Flossie Lewis became a teacher for a reason that history has made obsolete. "In the nineteen-forties if you were a girl, you *had* to go into teaching."

Florence Lewis's short stories and literary criticism have appeared in Commentary, Encounter, and The North American Review. Her husband plays string bass with the San Francisco Symphony.

30

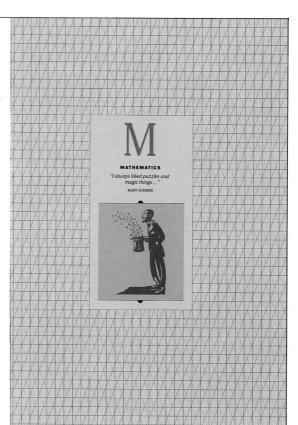

3.

M

MATHEMATICS
"I always liked puzzles and magic things…"
MARY SUNSERI

2.

Cover (1), spreads (2,3)

and spot illustration (4)

from product brochure

directed at wholesale

buyers.

DESIGN FIRM: Franek

Design Associates,

Washington, DC

DESIGNER: David Franek

PHOTOGRAPHER:

Ed Matalon

ILLUSTRATOR:

Jim Owens

Mobil
Petroleum products

COMMUNICATION FOR
MOTIVATION

The Wyatt Approach

1.

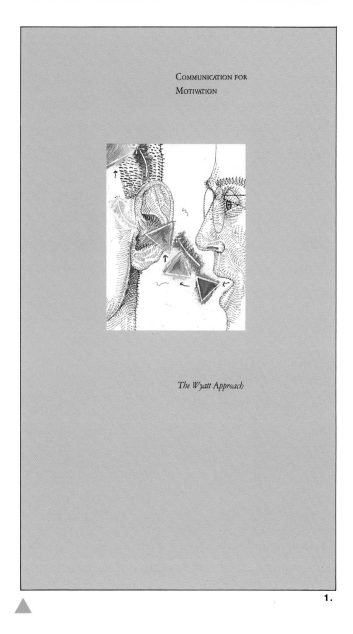

2.

3.

The Wyatt Company

Human resources communications consulting

Cover (1) and spreads

(2,3) from capabilities

brochure.

DESIGN FIRM: Liska &

Associates, Chicago,

Illinois

ART DIRECTOR:

Steven Liska

DESIGNER:

Susan Bennett

ILLUSTRATOR:

Alan E. Cober

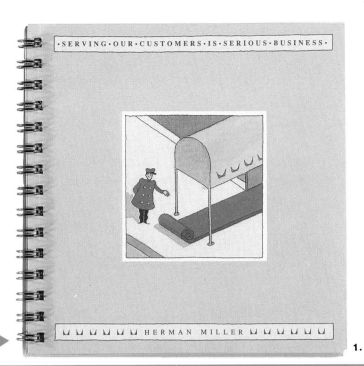

SERVING·OUR·CUSTOMERS·IS·SERIOUS·BUSINESS·

HERMAN MILLER

1.

Cover (1), spread (2) and illustrations (3,4,5) from promotional brochure for dealer service compaign.

DESIGNER: Linda Powell/ Herman Miller, Inc., Zeeland, Michigan

ILLUSTRATOR: Steven Guarnaccia

WRITER: Clark Malcolm

Herman Miller

Furniture

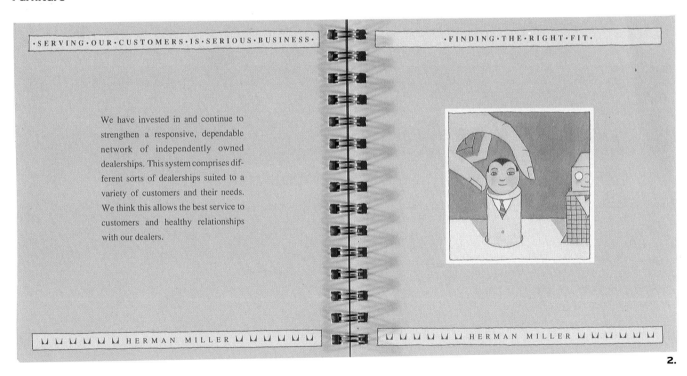

·SERVING·OUR·CUSTOMERS·IS·SERIOUS·BUSINESS·

·FINDING·THE·RIGHT·FIT·

We have invested in and continue to strengthen a responsive, dependable network of independently owned dealerships. This system comprises different sorts of dealerships suited to a variety of customers and their needs. We think this allows the best service to customers and healthy relationships with our dealers.

HERMAN MILLER

HERMAN MILLER

2.

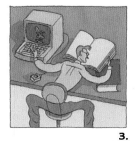

3.

4.

5.

1.

2.

Cover (2), spreads (3,4) and spot illustrations (5) from a promotional brochure designed to reposition the car and emphasize its luxury and safety rather than speed; cover (1) of sleeve/mailing envelope used for related direct-mail campaign.

DESIGN FIRM:

The Duffy Design Group, Minneapolis, Minnesota

ART DIRECTOR/ DESIGNER: Joe Duffy

ART DIRECTOR:

Haley Johnson

DESIGNER:

Charles S. Anderson

PHOTOGRAPHER:

Jeff Zwart

ILLUSTRATORS: Jan Evans, Lynn Schulte

Porsche

Automotive

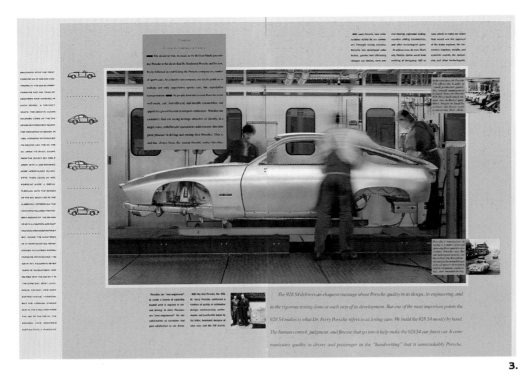

The 928 S4 delivers an eloquent message about Porsche quality in its design, its engineering, and in the rigorous testing done at each step of its development. But one of the most important points the 928 S4 makes is what Dr. Ferry Porsche refers to as loving care. We build the 928 S4 mostly by hand. The human control, judgment, and finesse that go into it help make the 928 S4 our finest car. It communicates quality to driver and passenger in the "handwriting" that is unmistakably Porsche.

3.

The 928 S4 is Porsche engineers' most sophisticated example of their ability to reposition the line that runs between automotive dream and automotive reality. As a result, it moves and feels like no other car. No matter how fast or slow you choose to drive, the 928 S4 retains its stability, poise, and distinctive character. Its smoothness through turns, under acceleration, or in a hard stop inspires well-founded confidence. The 928 S4 pays full tribute to the Porsche slogan, "Driving in its finest form."

4.

5.

A

B

C

Quality printing can be achieved with technology and skill. Quality service, however, can only be measured by the satisfaction of clients.

1.

If experience has taught you

to expect something less than

excellence from your printer,

chances are you have not done

business with Print Northwest.

We present these facts and observations for your consideration, and hope you will find them useful today and in the future.

2.

3.

Print Northwest

Printing

Sleeve (1), brochure cover (2), illustration (3) and spreads (4,5) from capabilities brochure announcing updated and expanded facilities and promoting the company as a "designer's" printer; piece introduced new identity featuring a changing "N".

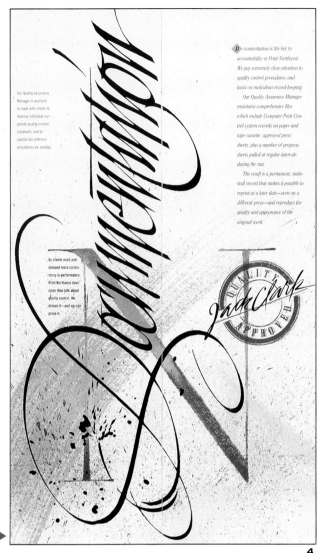

Our Quality Assurance Manager is available to meet with clients to develop individual corporate quality control standards; and to explore the different procedures we employ.

As clients need and demand more consistency in performance, Print Northwest does more than talk about quality control. We deliver it—and we can prove it.

D ocumentation is the key to accountability at Print Northwest. We pay extremely close attention to quality control procedures, and insist on meticulous record-keeping.

Our Quality Assurance Manager maintains comprehensive files which include Computer Print Control system records on paper and tape cassette, approved press sheets, plus a number of progress sheets pulled at regular intervals during the run.

The result is a permanent, statistical record that makes it possible to reprint at a later date—even on a different press—and reproduce the quality and appearance of the original work.

4.

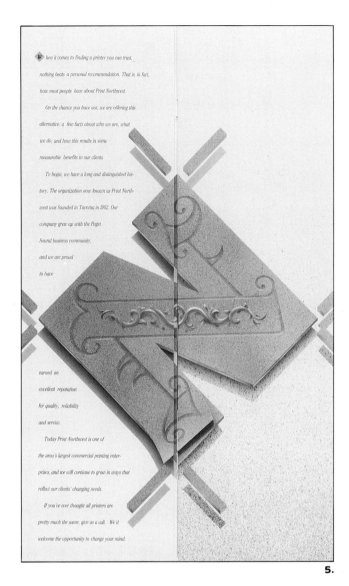

W hen it comes to finding a printer you can trust, nothing beats a personal recommendation. That is, in fact, how most people hear about Print Northwest.

On the chance you have not, we are offering this alternative: a few facts about who we are, what we do, and how this results in some measurable benefits to our clients.

To begin, we have a long and distinguished history. The organization now known as Print Northwest was founded in Tacoma in 1902. Our company grew up with the Puget Sound business community, and we are proud to have

earned an excellent reputation for quality, reliability and service.

Today Print Northwest is one of the area's largest commercial printing enterprises, and we will continue to grow in ways that reflect our clients' changing needs.

If you've ever thought all printers are pretty much the same, give us a call. We'd welcome the opportunity to change your mind.

5.

DESIGN FIRM: Hornall Anderson Design Works, Seattle, Washington

ART DIRECTOR/ DESIGNER: Jack Anderson

DESIGNERS: Heidi Hatlestad, Jani Drewfs

CALLIGRAPHERS: Georgia Deaver (4), Scott McDougall (3,5)

1.

Museum

Cover of pocket folder (1)

containing monthly

pages (2) for a

promotional calendar.

DESIGN FIRM: Ph.D.,

Santa Monica, California

DESIGNERS: Clive Piercy,

Michael Hodgson

ILLUSTRATOR:

Nancy Klobucar

2.

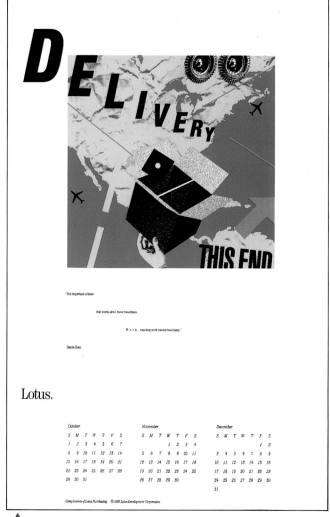

Sheets from promotional calendar mailed out quarterly to all Lotus vendors.

DESIGN FIRM: Forsythe Design, Cambridge, Massachusetts

ART DIRECTOR/ DESIGNER: Kathleen Forsythe

DESIGNERS: Julie Steinhilber, Jim Hood

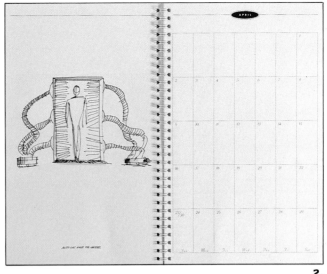

1.

2.

3.

4.

Capital Litho

Printing

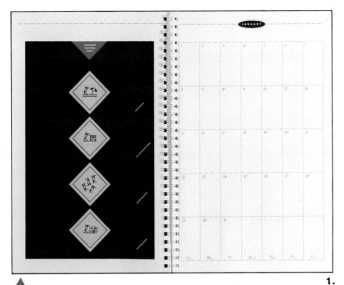

5.

Spreads (1,2,3,4) and spot illustration (5) from promotional desk calendar.
DESIGN FIRM: Ditko Design, Phoenix, Arizona
ART DIRECTOR/ DESIGNER: Steve Ditko

DESIGNERS/ ILLUSTRATORS: Smit, Ghormley Sanft (1), Dave Page (2), John Nelson (3), Robert Buzz Haynes and Jody Samuliner (4), Terry Bliss (5)

1.

2.

3.

CBS

Broadcasting

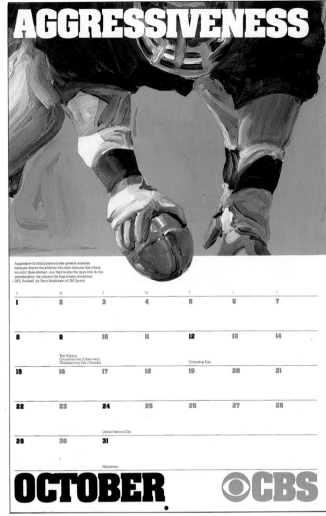

4.

5.

Cover (1), illustration (2) and spreads (3,4,5) from calendar promoting CBS's expertise in sports broadcasting and given away to callers of a 900 number.
DESIGN FIRM: Backer Spielvogel Bates

ART DIRECTOR:

Andrew Kner

ART DIRECTOR/

DESIGNER:

Lynda Decker

ILLUSTRATOR:

Tom Christopher

PCW Communications

Computer software

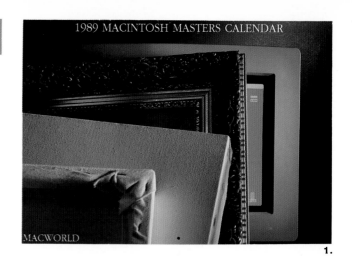

1.

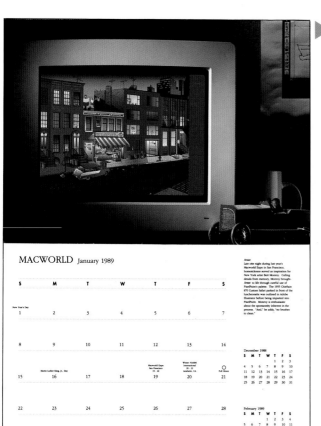

2.

3.

Cover (1) and spreads
(2,3) from promotional
calendar illustrating the
design possibilities on
computers.

DESIGN FIRM: Clement
Mok designs, San
Francisco, California

ART DIRECTOR:
Clement Mok

DESIGNERS: Dale
Horstman, Charles
Routhier

PHOTOGRAPHER:
John Greenleigh

1.

2.

3.

Basic American Medical

Health care

Cover (1) and spreads (2,3) from employee calendar featuring leaders in the company's corporate recognition program.

DESIGN FIRM: Marketing By Design, Greenwood, Indiana

DESIGNERS: Jim Butler, Nancy Peterson

ILLUSTRATORS: April Goodman-Willy (1), Susan Moore (2), Mario Noche (3)

CHILD'S PLAY

Kieffer Nolde

Electronic imaging

SEPTEMBER 1988

Kieffer-Nolde, Inc. Electronic Imaging for Print Communications 160 East Illinois Chicago Illinois 60611 312-337-5500 Toll Free 1-800-621-8214

kn

OCTOBER 1988

Kieffer-Nolde, Inc. Electronic Imaging for Print Communications 160 East Illinois Chicago Illinois 60611 312-337-5500 Toll Free 1-800-621-8214

kn

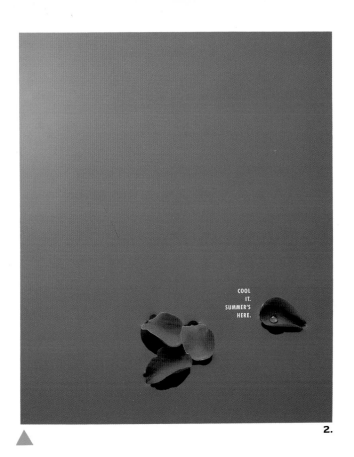

COOL
IT.
SUMMER'S
HERE.

2.

Covers (1,2) and spreads (3,4) from bimonthly promotional calendar series; steps for producing the images are on the back of each calendar.

DESIGN FIRM: Don Moravick & Associates, Chicago, Illinois

DESIGNER: Don Moravick

PHOTOGRAPHER: Dennis Manarchy

JULY 1988

AUGUST 1988

4.

1.

2.

Jerry Pavey/S&S Graphics Printing/S.D. Warren

Design and illustration/Printing/Paper products

5.

Cover (1), spreads (2,3,4) and art (5,6) from joint promotional calendar.

DESIGN FIRM: Jerry Pavey Design & Illustration, Silver Spring, Maryland

DESIGNER/ ILLUSTRATOR: Jerry Pavey

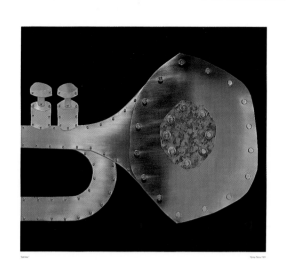

January

s	m	t	w	t	f	s
	1 *New Year's Day*	2	3	4	5	6
7	8	9	10	11	12	13
14	15 *Martin Luther King Day*	16	17	18	19	20
21	22	23	24	25	26	27
28	29	30	31			

3.

August

s	m	t	w	t	f	s
			1	2	3	4
5	6	7	8	9	10	11
12	13	14	15	16	17	18
19	20	21	22	23	24	25
26	27	28	29	30	31	

4.

6.

Broadcasting

1.

2.

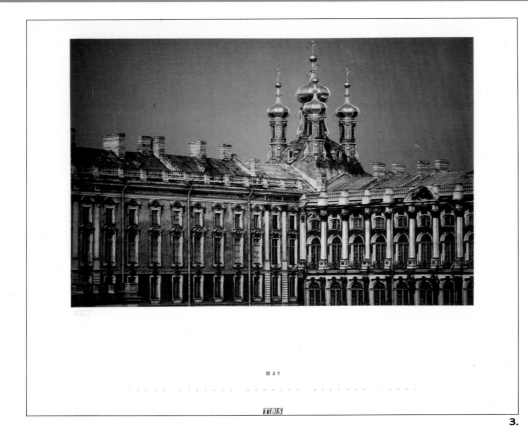

MAY

TBS

3.

Cover (1) and pages (2,3,4) from promotional calendar.

DESIGN FIRM: Executive Arts, Atlanta, Georgia

ART DIRECTOR: Buck Bell

DESIGNER: Phil Hamlett

PHOTOGRAPHER: Jim Brandenburg

PRINTER: The Hennegan Company

JULY

TBS

4.

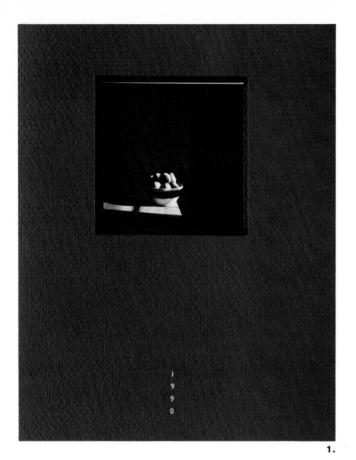

1.

Cover (1), spreads (2,4) and spread with open gatefold (3) from joint promotional calendar.

DESIGN FIRM:

Carbone Smolan,
New York, New York

ART DIRECTOR:

Leslie Smolan

DESIGNER:

Allison Muench

PHOTOGRAPHER:

Rodney Smith

2.

Design/Printing/Photography/Typesetting

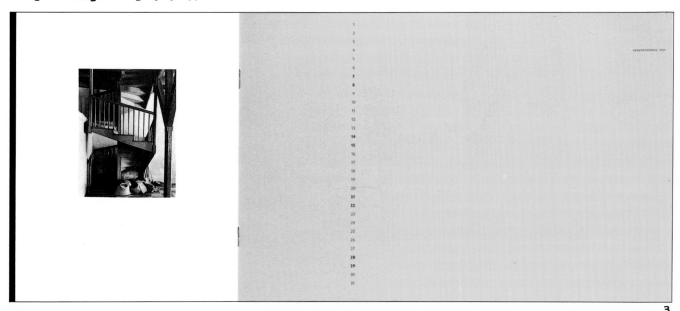

3.

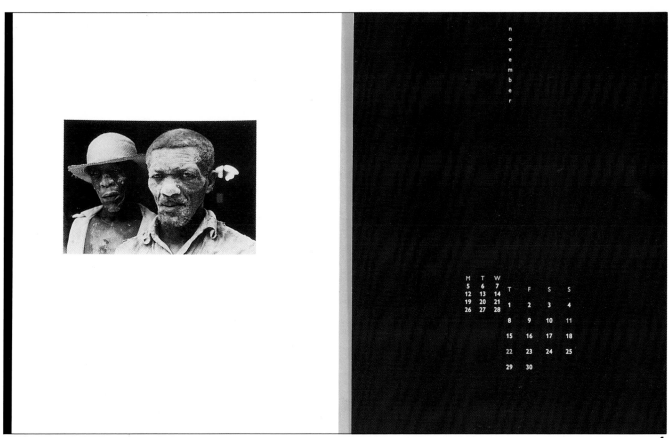

4.

1989

1.

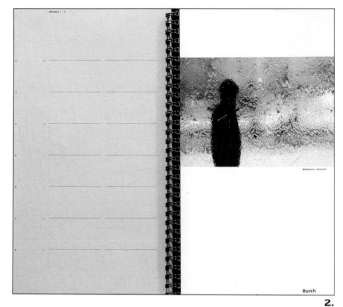

2.

3.

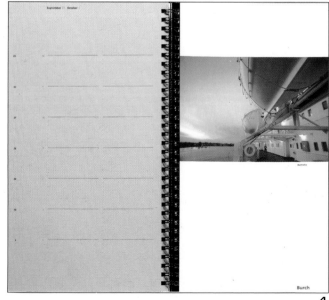

4.

Burch

Printing

Cover (1) and spreads

(2,3,4) from promotional

desk calendar.

DESIGN FIRM:

Liska and Associates,

Chicago, Illinois

DESIGNER: Steven Liska

PHOTOGRAPHER:

Tim Bieber,

Chicago, Illinois

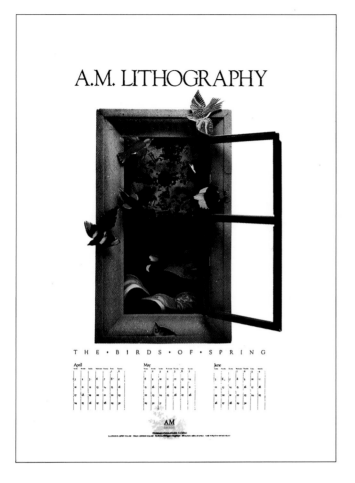

A.M. Lithography

Printing

Sheets from quarterly
promotional calendar
series drawing on the
"A.M." name for morning
themes.

DESIGN FIRM:

Pollard Design, East

Hartland, Connecticut

ART DIRECTOR/

ILLUSTRATOR:

Jeff Pollard

DESIGNER:

Adrienne Pollard

PHOTOGRAPHY:

Coon & Garrison

1.

2.

Spreads (1,2,3,4) and cover (5) of promotional calendar focusing on theme of "Outrageous ideas in print."

OVERALL DESIGNER: Kathleen Timmerman/ K.T.-White Space

INDIVIDUAL DESIGNERS: Lisa Jaroszynski and John Haines (2), Tim Simmons (3)

INDIVIDUAL ILLUSTRATORS/ DESIGNERS: Robin Feminella Olson (1), Mary Grand Pré (4)

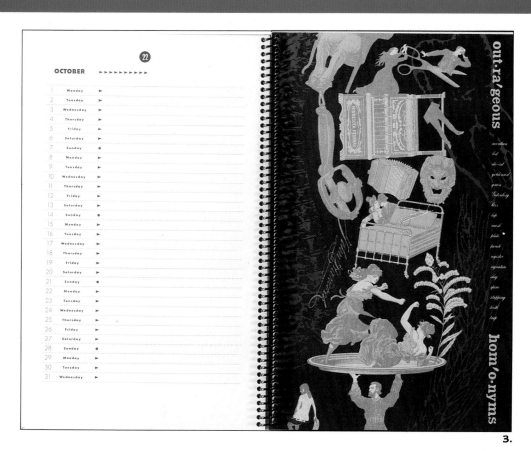

3.

5.

4.

Detail (1) and pages (2,3) from promotional calendar demonstrating potential of a new camera.

DESIGNER: Jeff Propper, Rockaway, New Jersey

PHOTOGRAPHER: Neil R. Molinaro, Clark, New Jersey

1.

SINAR AG Schaffhausen

Camera equipment

2.

3.

1.

2.

American President Companies

Shipping

Pages (1,2) and photo

(3) from promotional

wall calendar on the

subject of puzzles.

DESIGN FIRM:

Pentagram, San

Francisco, California

ART DIRECTOR/

DESIGNER: Kit Hinrichs

DESIGNER:

Sandra McHenry

PHOTOGRAPHER:

Terry Heffernan, San

Francisco, California

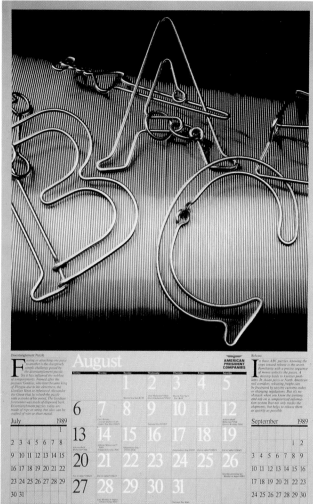

3.

1.

2.

California/International Arts Foundation
Non-profit arts foundation

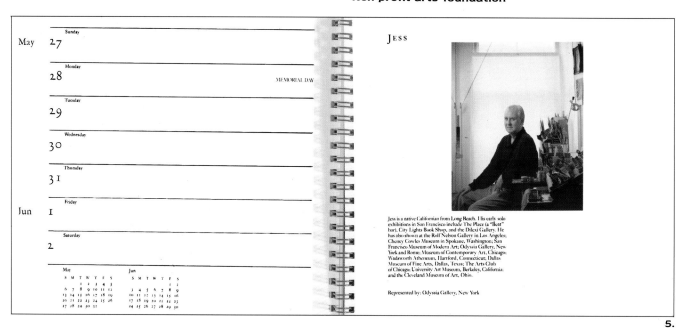

May 27 Sunday

28 Monday   MEMORIAL DAY

29 Tuesday

30 Wednesday

31 Thursday

Jun 1 Friday

2 Saturday

May
S M T W T F S
1 2 3 4 5
6 7 8 9 10 11 12
13 14 15 16 17 18 19
20 21 22 23 24 25 26
27 28 29 30 31

Jun
S M T W T F S
1 2
3 4 5 6 7 8 9
10 11 12 13 14 15 16
17 18 19 20 21 22 23
24 25 26 27 28 29 30

JESS

Jess is a native Californian from Long Beach. His early solo exhibitions in San Francisco include The Place (a "Beat" bar), City Lights Book Shop, and the Dilexi Gallery. He has also shown at the Rolf Nelson Gallery in Los Angeles; Cheney Cowles Museum in Spokane, Washington; San Francisco Museum of Modern Art; Odyssia Gallery, New York and Rome; Museum of Contemporary Art, Chicago; Wadsworth Atheneum, Hartford, Connecticut; Dallas Museum of Fine Arts, Dallas, Texas; The Arts Club of Chicago; University Art Museum, Berkeley, California; and the Cleveland Museum of Art, Ohio.

Represented by: Odyssia Gallery, New York

5.

Covers (1,2,3,4), spreads (5,6) and spot photo (7) from promotional/ fundraising calendar series promoting California artists.

DESIGN FIRM: The Graphics Studio, Los Angeles, California

DESIGNER: Gerry Rosentswieg

PHOTOGRAPHERS: Bill Miller (3,4), Victoria Miller (2), Jim McHugh (1,5) ARTISTS: Jess (6), Bruce Beasley (7)

3.

4.

JESS

"A Western Prospect of Egg and Dart" 1988
paste-up
56½" x 79¾"

Jun

	Sunday
3	
	Monday
4	
	Tuesday
5	
	Wednesday
6	
	Thursday
7	
	Friday
8	
	Saturday
9	

Jun							Jul						
S	M	T	W	T	F	S	S	M	T	W	T	F	S
					1	2							1
3	4	5	6	7	8	9	2	3	4	5	6	7	
10	11	12	13	14	15	16	8	9	10	11	12	13	14
17	18	19	20	21	22	23	15	16	17	18	19	20	21
24	25	26	27	28	29	30	22	23	24	25	26	27	28
							29	30	31				

6.

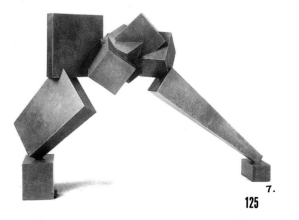

7.

1.

3.

2.

CREATIVE

the average man feels a sense of fear and mystery as he walks off the sand, into the surf zone. instinct is against it, and rightly so: a chest-high wave can knock down a clueless pedestrian with indifferent, breathtaking force. so we jones, on vacation in hawaii, or watching cable tv, might look at hawaiian michael ho dropping into a massive wave at waimea bay with the same reverence as he would the space shuttle charging into the dark blue of space, thinking, *what could that possibly be like?*

still, the audience for the sport of surfing and its byproduct activities is limited. common experience is the key to the mega-industrial sports of baseball, football and basketball. everyone's played; everyone can relate. surfing is opposite. the mainstream mind can't get a grip on an arena without chalk line markers, walls, or squared-off boundaries. on a competitive level, then, surfing is destined to remain a curiosity.

it's a fact that gives pause to professional surfers, skaters, snowboarders and the like. brock little, 22, lives and surfs on the north shore of oahu in hawaii, and sometimes imagines a parallel life in middle america "what if i had equal talent in another sport? *A sport sport?* what if i were just as good at, say, basketball as i am at surfing?" a short pause. "jeez, how much money would i be making then...?

there's no conceit in the remark, just idle curiosity, and an understanding of his position as surfing's premier utility man: slashing and quick in small-to-medium-size surf, in a league alone when the conditions get over 25'. this winter, surfing by himself a mile offshore, little rode a 30' wave, carving turns for 50 yards a stretch over a tilted blue-green field, the truck of his board disappearing into a mushroom cloud of whitewater. it was the biggest wave little had ridden in his life so far.

the money game is taken to the next level, as little weighs his blue-collar salary (paid largely by his clothing and wetsuit sponsors) against, say, a million-five as a ballplayer. but then he lists off a few nba cities — chicago, atlanta, new york ("... could be fun for a couple days"), boston, cleveland ("where's that, ohio? where's ohio?"), detroit and dallas — and the game's over. the idea of endlessly touring metropolitan america kills the million-dollar fantasy. the rhythm of brock little's life is locked to the rhythm of the north shore reefs: from banzai pipeline to sunset beach, waimea bay, himalayas and avalanche. he digs it on the frontier. he'll earn a decent wage and a big reputation in the years to come — and not give a shit about either one. the next time the surf is big enough to flood the highway and beat the pretenders back to higher ground, when it's 25' and rising, nothing matters to brock little but the drop.

4.

5.

Cover (3) and spreads (4,5) from seasonal clothing catalog designed to position the company as the leader in the "California" look; sleeve (1) and cover (2) of additional catalog.

DESIGN FIRM:
Mike Salisbury Communications, Torrance, California

ART DIRECTOR/ DESIGNER:
Mike Salisbury

DESIGNERS: Patrick O'Neal, Pam Hamilton, Scott Binkley, Ben Guerara, Terry Lamb, Pat Linse

PHOTOGRAPHER:
Mike Funk

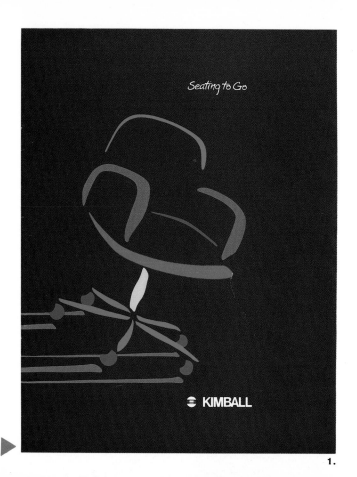

Seating to Go

≋ KIMBALL

1.

Casegoods to Go

≋ KIMBALL

2.

Kimball International

Furniture

3.

Cover (1), spread (3) and

spot illustration (4) from

product catalog; cover

(2) of additional catalog

in series.

DESIGNER/

ILLUSTRATOR:

Debra Holt/Kimball

International, Jasper,

Indiana

CREATIVE DIRECTOR:

Carol Skillman

4.

Cover (1) and spreads
(2,3) from catalog
introducing new furniture
collection.

DESIGNER: Bob Werner

AGENCY: Aves
Advertising, Inc., Grand
Rapids, Michigan

PHOTOGRAPHER:
Karl Francetic

Baker, Knapp & Tubbs

Furniture

1.

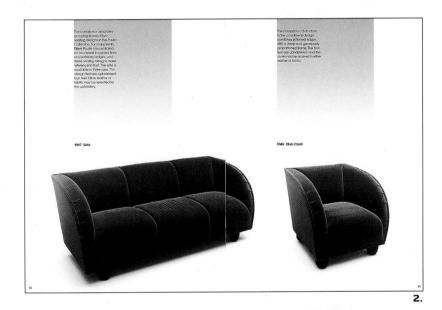

2.

3.

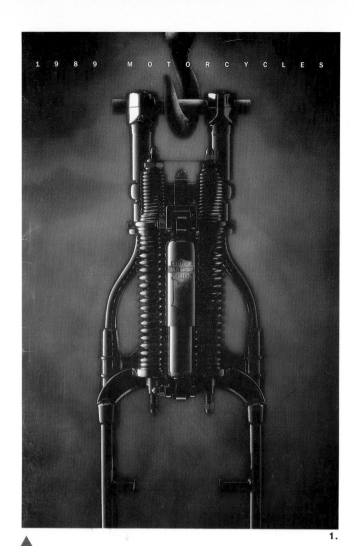

1989 MOTORCYCLES

1.

Cover (1) and spreads

(2,3) from 1989 dealer

catalog.

AGENCY:

Carmichael-Lynch

ART DIRECTOR:

David Page

PHOTOGRAPHER:

Aaron Jones, Santa Fe,

New Mexico

2.

3.

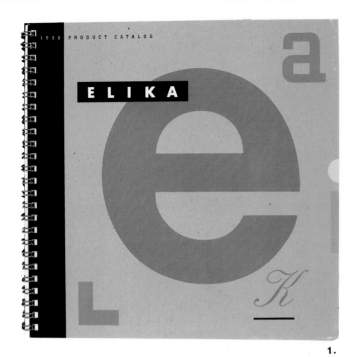

1.

Cover (1), spreads (2,3)

and spot photo (4) from

1990 product catalog.

DESIGN FIRM: Ph.D,

Santa Monica, California

DESIGNERS: Clive Piercy,

Michael Hodgson

2.

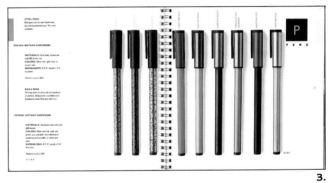

3.

Elika

Housewares

4.

Fine Writing Instruments for Corporate Recognition

· 1888 - 1988 ·

100 Years Dedicated to the Craft of Penmanship

⚕ PARKER

1.

2.

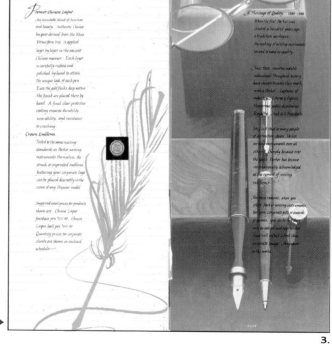

3.

Cover (1) and spreads (2,3) from marketing brochure for high-end product line.

DESIGN FIRM: Samata Associates, Dundee, Illinois

DESIGNERS: Pat and Greg Samata
ILLUSTRATOR: Kate Pagne

PHOTOGRAPHERS: Terry Heffernan, Dennis Dooley

Emergency guideline
manuals.
DESIGN FIRM: Vasa
Design, Avon,
Connecticut
DESIGNER: Natalie Vasa

Combustion Engineering

Engineering

Cover (1) and spreads (2,3) from catalog announcing opening of New York store.
DESIGNER: Tyler Smith, Providence, Rhode Island
FASHION PHOTOGRAPHY: John Goodman

ARCHITECTURAL PHOTOGRAPHY: Chris Maynard
COVER PHOTO: National Baseball Hall of Fame
COPYWRITER: Lee Nash

1.

Louis, Boston.

Clothing

2.

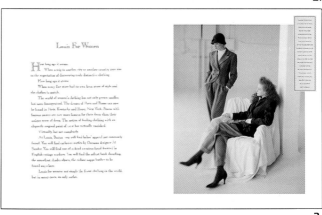

Louis For Women

3.

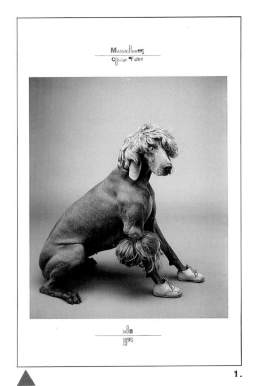

1.

Cover (1) and spreads

(2,3) from 1988/1990

catalog.

DESIGN FIRM: Schafer/

LaCasse Design,

Somerville,

Massachusetts

DESIGNERS: Sandra

Schafer, Bernard LaCasse

COVER PHOTO:

William Wegman

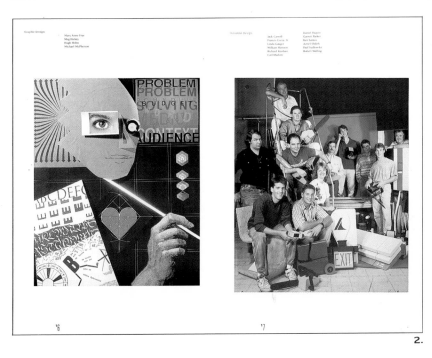

2.

3.

1.

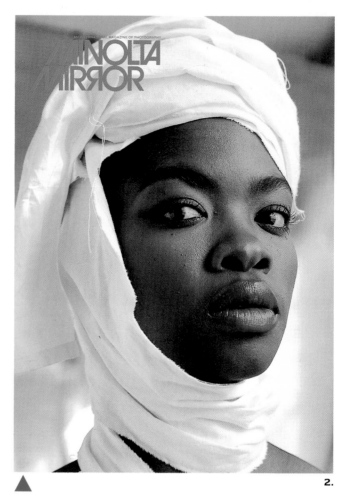

2.

Covers (1,2,3,4) and spreads (5,6,7) from corporate magazine given to customers via local distributors.

DESIGN FIRM: Bechlen/ Gonzalez, Inc., Honolulu, Hawaii

ART DIRECTOR/ DESIGNER: Fred Bechlen

PHOTOGRAPHER: Uwe Ommer

5.

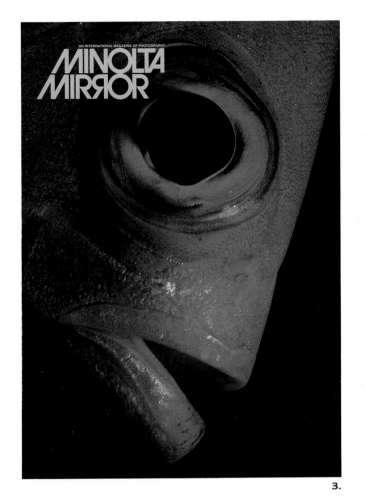

3.

4.

ABSTRACTS BY VAN ARSDALE

Photographer Nancy Van Arsdale uses a common household Minolta 16 and a battery of lenses...

Nancy Van Arsdale is a professional photographer who generally uses her nine Minolta SLR bodies and battery of lenses to shoot distinctive portraits, weddings, and a variety of other assignments, besides "fine-art" work—though she hates the term—for herself and clients.

Ms. Van Arsdale's interest in making camera abstracts was aroused by coincidence. One day several years ago a friend asked her to make some solid-color sheets to sandwich with transparencies of dancers. Nancy discovered that it would be more interesting to produce a series of abstract patterns instead. But what to use for subjects and how to shoot them? She began to search and experiment, in a few months cramming patterns as selected on these pages.

"I have tried all ways of making them," Nancy told me at Makubtion. "The

twirly or pour-like ones are fluids, which could be anything available almost in the kitchen, supermarket, or drugstore. For example, the only good ones I made last was egg tempera.

The start by pouring a few ounces of a "base" fluid, usually glycerin, corn syrup, or preservative, into a clear, clean proof glass lid from a baking dish. Then she adds a few flecks of varying colors and considers with an eyedropper...

camera meter. And exposures vary according to that heat challenging him. I'm lamp can break the good glass if left for too long. Nancy estimates it all sits foal at most one minute to shoot from the lens and a few I get. Colors are exaggerated by using Kodachrome 64 daylight type film with this back-related tungsten illumination.

"Other fluid combinations do no exist, but I'm squeezable them with a transpar work—just, or the mix of a tint, depending on the relative viscosity of the fluids involved at the relative want," Nancy explained.

6.   7.

137

Cover (1), spread (3) and diagrams (4,6) from corporate magazine; spread (5) and spot illustration (2) from a different issue.

DESIGN FIRM: SHR Design Communications, Scottsdale, Arizona

ART DIRECTOR/ DESIGNER:

Miles Abernethy

ART DIRECTOR:

Barry Shepard

DESIGNERS: Doug Reeder, Karin Burklein Arnold

ILLUSTRATORS: James Endicott (2), Carol Hughes (4)

PHOTOGRAPHER:

Rick Rusing (4)

COPYWRITER:

Steve Hutchinson

1.

2.

Audi
Automotive

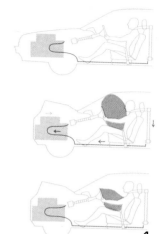

4.

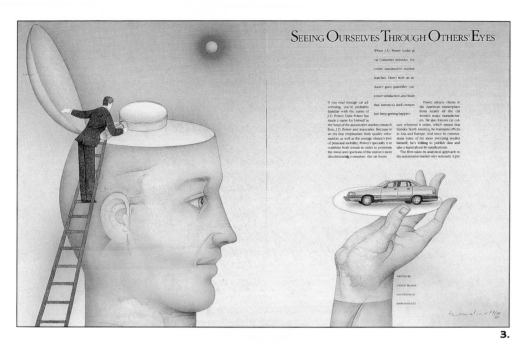

Seeing Ourselves Through Others' Eyes

When J.D. Power looks at car consumer attitudes, the entire automotive market watches. Here's how an industry guru quantifies customer satisfaction, and finds that America's Audi owners just keep getting happier.

If you read enough car advertising, you're probably familiar with the name of J.D. Power. Dave Power has made a name for himself as the head of the automotive market-research firm, J.D. Power and Associates. Because in an era that emphasizes both quality information, as well as the average citizen's love of personal mobility, Power's specialty is to combine both trends in order to penetrate the mind and opinions of the nation's most discriminating consumer: the car buyer.

Power attracts clients in the American marketplace from nearly all the car world's major manufacturers. He also follows car culture wherever it exists, which means that besides North America, he maintains offices in Asia and Europe. And since he commissions some of his most sweeping studies himself, he's willing to publish data and take a stand about its ramifications.

The firm takes its analytical approach to the automotive market very seriously. A pri-

WRITTEN BY
LINDSAY BRObAN

ILLUSTRATED BY
JAMES ENDICOTT

3.

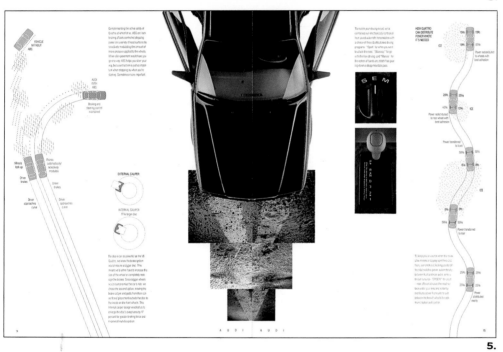

5.

3-Year 50,000 Mile Limited Warranty

Roadside Assistance 5

New Audi Purchase

Audi Maintenance Protection

Guaranteed Resale Index

10-Year Corrosion Perforation Warranty

6.

1.

Cover (2), spread (4) and spot illustrations (1,3) from issue of alumni magazine; covers (5,7) and spreads (6,8) from additional issues.

DESIGN FIRM: Gerhardt & Clemons, Inc., Chicago, Illinois

ART DIRECTOR:

Carol Gerhardt

DESIGNERS: Christine Celano, Barbara Rohm

ILLUSTRATORS: Steve Johnson, Michael Swain, Linden Wilson, Tom Curry, Andrzej Dudzinski, Mary Flock, Lane Smith, Scott Wright, Jeff Meyer, Chris Sheban

GSB

Chicago

The University of Chicago Graduate School of Business

Vol. 12 No. 1 | Spring 1989

2.

3.

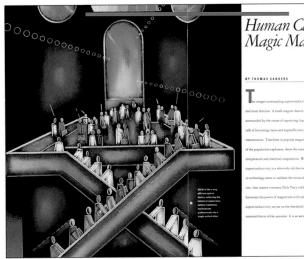

Human Capital and Magic Machines

BY THOMAS SANDERS

The images surrounding superconductivity are becoming more and more familiar. A small magnet dances above a horizontal disk surrounded by the steam of vaporizing liquid nitrogen. Visionaries talk of levitating trains and superefficient energy production and transmission. Timelines in popular magazines, looking like charts of the population explosion, show the course of breakthroughs in temperature and material composition. While the phenomenon of superconductivity is a relatively old discovery, recent developments in technology seem to validate the miraculous claims. In the sixties, that master visionary Dick Tracy told us, "The country that harnesses the power of magnetism will rule the world." With superconductivity we are on the threshold of taming one of the essential forces of the universe. It is an astonishing thought.

4.

5.

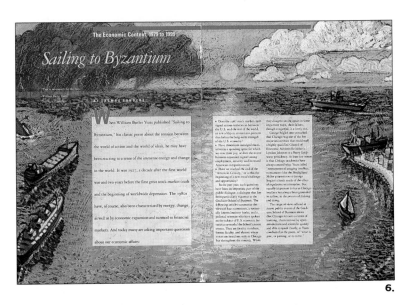

The Economic Context, 1979 to 1999

Sailing to Byzantium

BY THOMAS SANDERS

When William Butler Yeats published "Sailing to Byzantium," his classic poem about the tension between the world of action and the world of ideas, he may have been reacting to a sense of the immense energy and change in the world. It was 1927, a decade after the first world war and two years before the first great stock market crash and the beginning of worldwide depression. The 1980s have, of course, also been characterized by energy, change, as well as by economic expansion and turmoil in financial markets. And today many are asking important questions about our economic affairs:

6.

7.

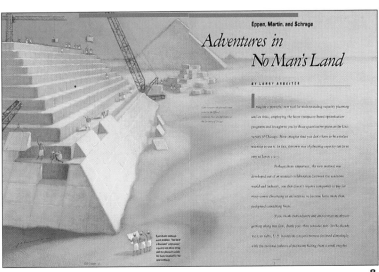

Eppen, Martin, and Schrage

Adventures in No Man's Land

BY LARRY ARBEITER

Imagine a powerful new tool for wide-ranging capacity planning and analysis, employing the latest computer-based optimization programs and brought to you by those quantitative gurus at the University of Chicago. Now imagine that you don't have to be a rocket scientist to use it. In fact, this new way of planning capacity can be as easy as Lotus 1-2-3.

8.

PRISM

Summer 1989

Arthur D Little

**Harnessing Technology
as a Strategic Asset**

Plus: 3M's William DeGenaro
on Encouraging Innovation

1.

PRISM

Second Quarter 1990

Arthur D Little

**Risk, Uncertainty, and Crisis:
The Changing Context
of Management**

2.

Covers (1,2), spread (3)
and illustrations (4,5)
from quarterly magazine
sent to current and
potential clients.
**DESIGN FIRM: Sametz/
Blackstone Associates,
Boston, Massachusetts**

ART DIRECTOR:

Roger Sametz

DESIGNER:

Stuart Darsch

ILLUSTRATOR:

Richard A. Goldberg

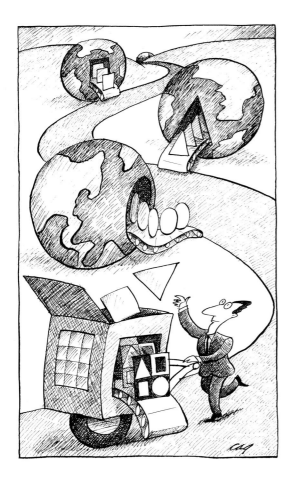

Sourcing Technology:
New Challenges,
Innovative Solutions

John M. Ketteringham and Stephen E. Rudolph

Faced with the triple challenges of increasing product sophistication, intensifying competition, and global proliferation of technology development, most companies can no longer develop internally all the technologies they need. Increasingly, they must pursue technology aggressively as a strategic component of their business and must source it worldwide.

For most of this century, major companies have grown and prospered largely on the basis of internal investments in technology. Today, however, increasing product sophistication is making it difficult for companies to continue to develop internally all the technologies they need to be successful. Furthermore, increasing competitive intensity has made time a critical variable. Perhaps most significantly, the proliferation of technology development on a global scale is forcing dramatic changes in technology development and acquisition. In this article we examine the likely effects of each of these trends on the ways companies will conduct product development.

The Objectives of Product Development

The basic objectives of product development are shared across many product categories. These include creating the right products, incorporating appropriate technology, offering the highest possible quality at the lowest possible cost, and introducing each product at the right time.[1]

Creating the Right Products. The right products are those that meet the needs and wishes of targeted customers. They must be attractively designed and easy to operate, as well as up to date in performance and features. Furthermore, they must be clearly and advantageously differentiated from competitors' products.

5   Arthur D. Little

3.

4.

5.

VOLUME 2 NUMBER 1 1990

VIEWs

LEADING-EDGE IDEAS FOR THOSE WHO SHAPE AMERICA'S COMMERCE, INDUSTRY, RESORTS, AND RESIDENCES

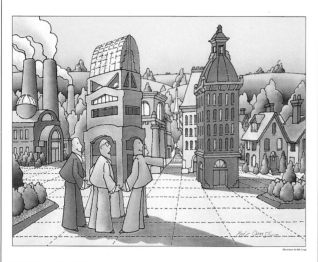

Illustration by Bob Conge

Novel Approaches to Planning Strengthen Development Futures

A large western basin faces intense development pressures head on. A burgeoning northeast commercial district struggles with traffic congestion impacting a wide geographic area. A small lakeside community fights to overcome demographic shifts which

have left it with a dwindling population and tax base. And a thriving northern suburb begins the process of updating an outdated, outmoded master plan.

What do these areas have in common? In each place, groups are turning to novel approaches to deal with planning and growth issues. And developers, once the guys wearing the black hats, are being invited into the process.

Planning is gaining recognition and urgency as land use issues—once debated only in the back rooms at

city hall—are increasingly the subject of public debate.

"Times certainly have changed," says Cris Schulz, administrative assistant to the County Commissioners in Summit County, Utah. "You get shot out of the saddle if you try to plan in the back room. Today, planning issues are front page news. They are big issues—issues which can bring communities together, or tear them apart."

Schulz coordinated an innovative planning session in Utah to hammer out future development options

1.

VOLUME 1 NUMBER 4 1989

VIEWs

LEADING-EDGE IDEAS FOR THOSE WHO SHAPE AMERICA'S COMMERCE, INDUSTRY, RESORTS, AND RESIDENCES

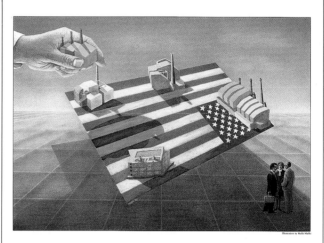

Illustrations by Malik Malik

 ## Industrial Space Needs Changing

A basic restructuring of America's industrial sector has been underway now for about 15 or 20 years. In the aggregate, little has changed. We employ almost exactly the same number of people in manufacturing that we did 20 years ago. But underneath that aggregate lies a fascinating story.

Since 1980, the Fortune 500 that employed about 78 percent of all manufacturing workers in 1980 have restructured and downsized to an extent few of us would have dreamed possible at the beginning of

the decade. By the end of 1987 they employed 3.1 million fewer people than they had at the beginning of 1980. That's the equivalent of the entire workforce, public and private, of Massachusetts.

But overall manufacturing employment has not declined by nearly that amount. In fact, by the end of 1987 it had fallen by only 1.2 million. The non-Fortune 500 part of the industrial economy, beginning the decade with only 22 percent of its workforce, has compensated for almost two-thirds of the Fortune 500 losses.

In addition, as we trade more, we distribute more. The distribution sector of the economy has been booming. These two trends—the restructuring of manufacturing and growth in distribution—are cre-

ating a significant need for industrial space in the United States, even at a time when many places are experiencing a huge glut of office space.

One of the keys to the need for industrial space is its lack of interchangeability. A candy factory is not easily converted into a textile mill. An unneeded automobile plant does not cost-effectively serve the needs of a growing bakery. Even in distribution, an older facility may not be an adequate substitute for the cool, or dry, dust-free environment required by a new electronics company. In short, unlike office space, which can be used interchangeably by most office dwellers, much of the need for new industrial space cannot be met by existing facilities. Thus we experience continuous construction of industrial space

2.

Covers (1,2), spread (3) and spot illustration (4) from quarterly corporate newsletter.

DESIGN FIRM:

Conge Design, Rochester, New York

ART DIRECTOR:

Chris Cook

DESIGNER/

ILLUSTRATOR:

Bob Conge

Sear-Brown Group

Engineering

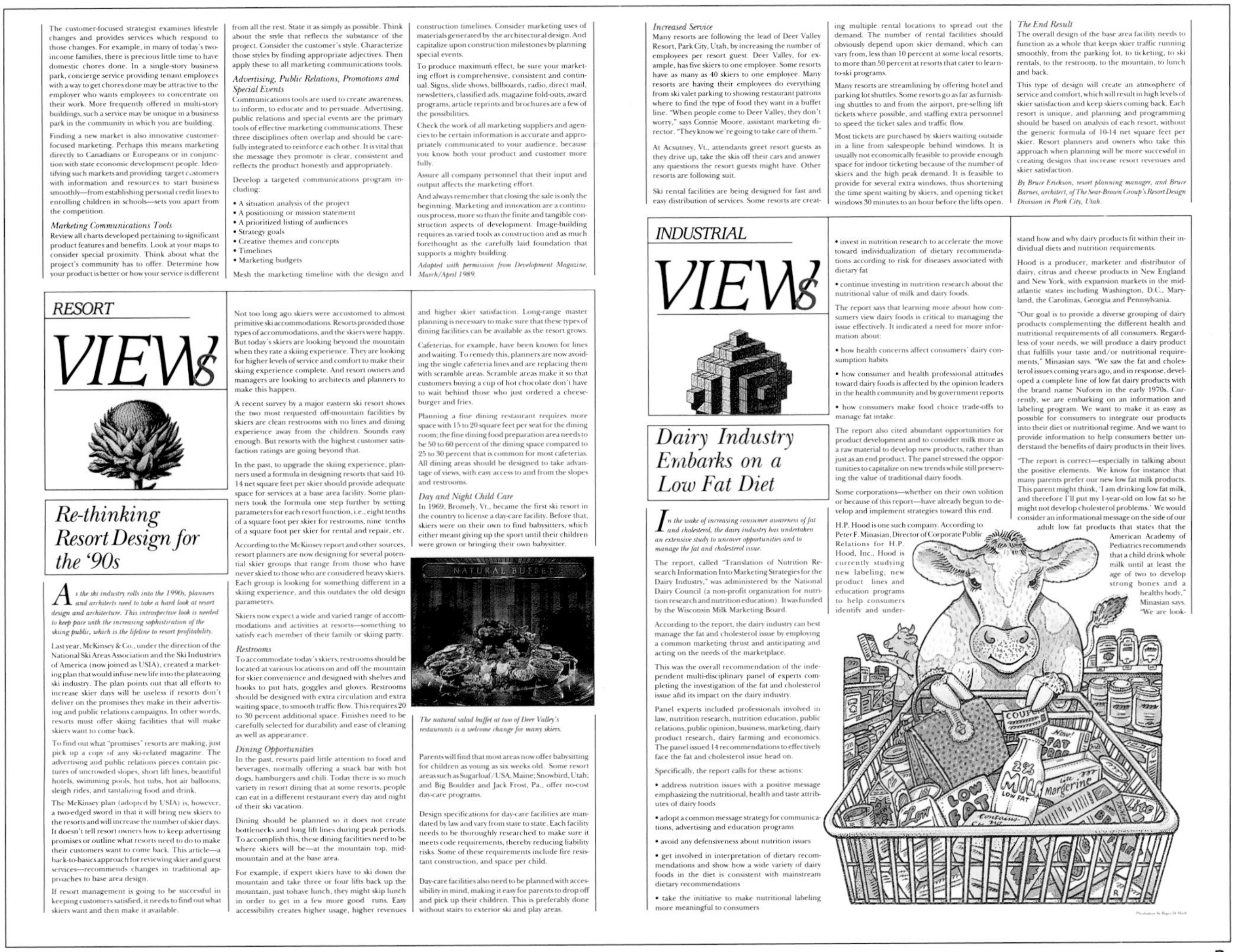

The customer-focused strategist examines lifestyle changes and provides services which respond to those changes. For example, in many of today's two-income families, there is precious little time to have domestic chores done. In a single-story business park, concierge service providing tenant employees with a way to get chores done may be attractive to the employer who wants employees to concentrate on their work. More frequently offered in multi-story buildings, such a service may be unique in a business park in the community in which you are building.

Finding a new market is also innovative customer-focused marketing. Perhaps this means marketing directly to Canadians or Europeans or in conjunction with state economic development people. Identifying such markets and providing target customers with information and resources to start business smoothly—from establishing personal credit lines to enrolling children in schools—sets you apart from the competition.

Marketing Communications Tools

Review all charts developed pertaining to significant product features and benefits. Look at your maps to consider special proximity. Think about what the project's community has to offer. Determine how your product is better or how your service is different from all the rest. State it as simply as possible. Think about the style that reflects the substance of the project. Consider the customer's style. Characterize those styles by finding appropriate adjectives. Then apply these to all marketing communications tools.

Advertising, Public Relations, Promotions and Special Events

Communications tools are used to create awareness, to inform, to educate and to persuade. Advertising, public relations and special events are the primary tools of effective marketing communications. These three disciplines often overlap and should be carefully integrated to reinforce each other. It is vital that the message they promote is clear, consistent and reflects the product honestly and appropriately.

Develop a targeted communications program including:

- A situation analysis of the project
- A positioning or mission statement
- A prioritized listing of audiences
- Strategy goals
- Creative themes and concepts
- Timelines
- Marketing budgets

Mesh the marketing timeline with the design and construction timelines. Consider marketing uses of materials generated by the architectural design. And capitalize upon construction milestones by planning special events.

To produce maximum effect, be sure your marketing effort is comprehensive, consistent and continual. Signs, slide shows, billboards, radio, direct mail, newsletters, classified ads, magazine fold-outs, award programs, article reprints and brochures are a few of the possibilities.

Check the work of all marketing suppliers and agencies to be certain information is accurate and appropriately communicated to your audience, because you know both your product and customer more fully.

Assure all company personnel that their input and output affects the marketing effort.

And always remember that closing the sale is only the beginning. Marketing and innovation are a continuous process, more so than the finite and tangible construction aspects of development. Image-building requires as varied tools as construction and as much forethought as the carefully laid foundation that supports a mighty building.

Adapted with permission from Development Magazine, March/April 1989.

RESORT

VIEWS

Re-thinking Resort Design for the '90s

As the ski industry rolls into the 1990s, planners and architects need to take a hard look at resort design and architecture. This introspective look is needed to keep pace with the increasing sophistication of the skiing public, which is the lifeline to resort profitability.

Last year, McKinsey & Co., under the direction of the National Ski Areas Association and the Ski Industries of America (now joined as USIA), created a marketing plan that would infuse new life into the plateauing ski industry. The plan points out that all efforts to increase skier days will be useless if resorts don't deliver on the promises they make in their advertising and public relations campaigns. In other words, resorts must offer skiing facilities that will make skiers want to come back.

To find out what "promises" resorts are making, just pick up a copy of any ski-related magazine. The advertising and public relations pieces contain pictures of uncrowded slopes, short lift lines, beautiful hotels, swimming pools, hot tubs, hot air balloons, sleigh rides, and tantalizing food and drink.

The McKinsey plan (adopted by USIA) is, however, a two-edged sword in that it will bring new skiers to the resorts and will increase the number of skier days. It doesn't tell resort owners how to keep advertising promises or outline what resorts need to do to make their customers want to come back. This article—a back-to-basics approach for reviewing skier and guest services—recommends changes in traditional approaches to base area design.

If resort management is going to be successful in keeping customers satisfied, it needs to find out what skiers want and then make it available.

Not too long ago skiers were accustomed to almost primitive ski accommodations. Resorts provided those types of accommodations, and the skiers were happy. But today's skiers are looking beyond the mountain when they rate a skiing experience. They are looking for higher levels of service and comfort to make their skiing experience complete. And resort owners and managers are looking to architects and planners to make this happen.

A recent survey by a major eastern ski resort shows the two most requested off-mountain facilities by skiers are clean restrooms with no lines and dining experience away from the children. Sounds easy enough. But resorts with the highest customer satisfaction ratings are going beyond that.

In the past, to upgrade the skiing experience, planners used a formula in designing resorts that said 10-14 net square feet per skier should provide adequate space for services at a base area facility. Some planners took the formula one step further by setting parameters for each resort function, i.e., eight tenths of a square foot per skier for restrooms, nine tenths of a square foot per skier for rental and repair, etc.

According to the McKinsey report and other sources, resort planners are now designing for several potential skier groups that range from those who have never skied to those who are considered heavy skiers. Each group is looking for something different in a skiing experience, and this outdates the old design parameters.

Skiers now expect a wide and varied range of accommodations and activities at resorts—something to satisfy each member of their family or skiing party.

Restrooms

To accommodate today's skiers, restrooms should be located at various locations on and off the mountain for skier convenience and designed with shelves and hooks to put hats, goggles and gloves. Restrooms should be designed with extra circulation and extra waiting space, to smooth traffic flow. This requires 20 to 30 percent additional space. Finishes need to be carefully selected for durability and ease of cleaning as well as appearance.

Dining Opportunities

In the past, resorts paid little attention to food and beverages, normally offering a snack bar with hot dogs, hamburgers and chili. Today there is so much variety in resort dining that at some resorts, people can eat in a different restaurant every day and night of their ski vacation.

Dining should be planned so it does not create bottlenecks and long lift lines during peak periods. To accomplish this, these dining facilities need to be where skiers will be—at the mountain top, mid-mountain and at the base area.

For example, if expert skiers have to ski down the mountain and take three or four lifts back up the mountain, just tohave lunch, they might skip lunch in order to get in a few more good runs. Easy accessibility creates higher usage, higher revenues and higher skier satisfaction. Long-range master planning is necessary to make sure that these types of dining facilities can be available as the resort grows.

Cafeterias, for example, have been known for lines and waiting. To remedy this, planners are now avoiding the single cafeteria lines and are replacing them with scramble areas. Scramble areas make it so that customers buying a cup of hot chocolate don't have to wait behind those who just ordered a cheeseburger and fries.

Planning a fine dining restaurant requires more space with 15 to 20 square feet per seat for the dining room; the fine dining food preparation area needs to be 50 to 60 percent of the dining space compared to 25 to 30 percent that is common for most cafeterias. All dining areas should be designed to take advantage of views, with easy access to and from the slopes and restrooms.

Day and Night Child Care

In 1969, Bromely, Vt., became the first ski resort in the country to license a day-care facility. Before that, skiers were on their own to find babysitters, which either meant giving up the sport until their children were grown or bringing their own babysitter.

NATURAL BUFFET

The natural salad buffet at two of Deer Valley's restaurants is a welcome change for many skiers.

Parents will find that most areas now offer babysitting for children as young as six weeks old. Some resort areas such as Sugarloaf/USA, Maine; Snowbird, Utah; and Big Boulder and Jack Frost, Pa., offer no-cost day-care programs.

Design specifications for day-care facilities are mandated by law and vary from state to state. Each facility needs to be thoroughly researched to make sure it meets code requirements, thereby reducing liability risks. Some of these requirements include fire resistant construction, and space per child.

Day-care facilities also need to be planned with accessibility in mind, making it easy for parents to drop off and pick up their children. This is preferably done without stairs to exterior ski and play areas.

Increased Service

Many resorts are following the lead of Deer Valley Resort, Park City, Utah, by increasing the number of employees per resort guest. Deer Valley, for example, has five skiers to one employee. Some resorts have as many as 40 skiers to one employee. Many resorts are having their employees do everything from ski valet parking to showing restaurant patrons where to find the type of food they want in a buffet line. "When people come to Deer Valley, they don't worry," says Connie Moore, assistant marketing director. "They know we're going to take care of them."

At Acsutney, Vt., attendants greet resort guests as they drive up, take the skis off their cars and answer any questions the resort guests might have. Other resorts are following suit.

Ski rental facilities are being designed for fast and easy distribution of services. Some resorts are creating multiple rental locations to spread out the demand. The number of rental facilities should obviously depend upon skier demand, which can vary from, less than 10 percent at some local resorts, to more than 50 percent at resorts that cater to learn-to-ski programs.

Many resorts are streamlining by offering hotel and parking lot shuttles. Some resorts go as far as furnishing shuttles to and from the airport, pre-selling lift tickets where possible, and staffing extra personnel to speed the ticket sales and traffic flow.

Most tickets are purchased by skiers waiting outside in a line from salespeople behind windows. It is usually not economically feasible to provide enough space for indoor ticketing because of the number of skiers and the high peak demand. It is feasible to provide for several extra windows, thus shortening the time spent waiting by skiers, and opening ticket windows 30 minutes to an hour before the lifts open.

The End Result

The overall design of the base area facility needs to function as a whole that keeps skier traffic running smoothly, from the parking lot, to ticketing, to ski rentals, to the restroom, to the mountain, to lunch and back.

This type of design will create an atmosphere of service and comfort, which will result in high levels of skier satisfaction and keep skiers coming back. Each resort is unique, and planning and programming should be based on analysis of each resort, without the generic formula of 10-14 net square feet per skier. Resort planners and owners who take this approach when planning will be more successful in creating designs that increase resort revenues and skier satisfaction.

By Bruce Erickson, resort planning manager, and Bruce Barnes, architect, of The Sear-Brown Group's Resort Design Division in Park City, Utah.

INDUSTRIAL

VIEWS

Dairy Industry Embarks on a Low Fat Diet

In the wake of increasing consumer awareness of fat and cholesterol, the dairy industry has undertaken an extensive study to uncover opportunities and to manage the fat and cholesterol issue.

The report, called "Translation of Nutrition Research Information Into Marketing Strategies for the Dairy Industry," was administered by the National Dairy Council (a non-profit organization for nutrition research and nutrition education). It was funded by the Wisconsin Milk Marketing Board.

According to the report, the dairy industry can best manage the fat and cholesterol issue by employing a common marketing thrust and anticipating and acting on the needs of the marketplace.

This was the overall recommendation of the independent multi-disciplinary panel of experts completing the investigation of the fat and cholesterol issue and its impact on the dairy industry.

Panel experts included professionals involved in law, nutrition research, nutrition education, public relations, public opinion, business, marketing, dairy product research, dairy farming and economics. The panel issued 14 recommendations to effectively face the fat and cholesterol issue head on.

Specifically, the report calls for these actions:

- address nutrition issues with a positive message emphasizing the nutritional, health and taste attributes of dairy foods
- adopt a common message strategy for communications, advertising and education programs
- avoid any defensiveness about nutrition issues
- get involved in interpretation of dietary recommendations and show how a wide variety of dairy foods in the diet is consistent with mainstream dietary recommendations
- take the initiative to make nutritional labeling more meaningful to consumers
- invest in nutrition research to accelerate the move toward individualization of dietary recommendations according to risk for diseases associated with dietary fat
- continue investing in nutrition research about the nutritional value of milk and dairy foods.

The report says that learning more about how consumers view dairy foods is critical to managing the issue effectively. It indicated a need for more information about:

- how health concerns affect consumers' dairy consumption habits
- how consumer and health professional attitudes toward dairy foods is affected by the opinion leaders in the health community and by government reports
- how consumers make food choice trade-offs to manage fat intake.

The report also cited abundant opportunities for product development and to consider milk more as a raw material to develop new products, rather than just as an end product. The panel stressed the opportunities to capitalize on new trends while still preserving the value of traditional dairy foods.

Some corporations—whether on their own volition or because of this report—have already begun to develop and implement strategies toward this end.

H.P. Hood is one such company. According to Peter F. Minasian, Director of Corporate Public Relations for H.P. Hood, Inc., Hood is currently studying new labeling, new product lines and education programs to help consumers identify and understand how and why dairy products fit within their individual diets and nutrition requirements.

Hood is a producer, marketer and distributor of dairy, citrus and cheese products in New England and New York, with expansion markets in the mid-atlantic states including Washington, D.C., Maryland, the Carolinas, Georgia and Pennsylvania.

"Our goal is to provide a diverse grouping of dairy products complementing the different health and nutritional requirements of all consumers. Regardless of your needs, we will produce a dairy product that fulfills your taste and/or nutritional requirements," Minasian says. "We saw the fat and cholesterol issues coming years ago, and in response, developed a complete line of low fat dairy products with the brand name Nuform in the early 1970s. Currently, we are embarking on an information and labeling program. We want to make it as easy as possible for consumers to integrate our products into their diet or nutritional regime. And we want to provide information to help consumers better understand the benefits of dairy products in their lives.

"The report is correct—especially in talking about the positive elements. We know for instance that many parents prefer our new low fat milk products. This parent might think, 'I am drinking low fat milk, and therefore I'll put my 1-year-old on low fat so he might not develop cholesterol problems.' We would consider an informational message on the side of our adult low fat products that states that the American Academy of Pediatrics recommends that a child drink whole milk until at least the age of two to develop strong bones and a healthy body," Minasian says. "We are look-

3.

4.

Illustration by David Cowles

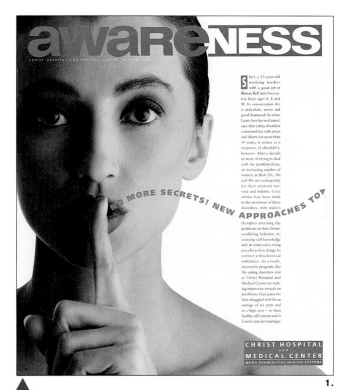

1.

2.

Covers (1,2) and spreads (3,4) from quarterly consumer information magazine.

CREATIVE DIRECTOR:

Nancy Tait

ART DIRECTORS/

DESIGNERS: Mark

Feldman, Lakshmi

Narayan-Burns/Creative

Services Group,

Evangelical Health

Systems, Oak Brook,

Illinois

PHOTOGRAPHER:

Eric Herzog (1,2)

Multi-dimensional Treatment Approach. Self-awareness and understanding—these are the key elements to the program's three-pronged treatment approach. "We help patients find alternative ways of thinking about themselves, food and weight," says Minal Patel, M.D., program coordinator of Christ Hospital and Medical Center's eating disorders unit. "Through individual and group therapy, we identify the feelings that trigger the problem behavior, and nurture new skills for understanding and coping with these feelings." The second aspect of treatment is helping patients break their food-related rituals. In addition to practicing normal three-meals-a-day eating, they relearn skills like meal preparation and eating in restaurants and social situations. At one point, patients share a meal with their families, which the staff observes and discusses afterward. A dietitian works with each patient to develop a healthy, balanced eating plan involving menus he or she can maintain comfortably—without fear of gaining excess weight. For many patients, a third component of treatment is the use of medications. Anorexics and bulimics often can be helped with antianxiety drugs and antidepressants—even if they aren't depressed or suffering from anxiety disorders.

Researchers Seek Clues to a Complex Problem. Researchers aren't certain why these medications work. Nor do they know precisely what causes eating disorders in the first place. But one study

OVERCOMING THE STRESS AND SHAME OF EATING DISORDERS

suggests that a significant biochemical malfunction may lie behind the behavioral abnormality. Reported in the newsweekly *Science News*, the study found that bulimics fail to secrete normal amounts of a hormone called cholecystokinin (CCK) that induces a sense of satiety or fullness after a meal. Another study has shown that after taking antidepressants for eight weeks, the bulimic's CCK response seems to be restored. As the researchers themselves have pointed out, however, it's doubtful that just one body chemical controls a behavior as complex as eating. More likely, the source of these problems lies in a subtle blend of cultural, genetic and personal factors as well as biochemistry.

The other probable influences in eating disorders? Genes may be a predisposing factor, with upbringing and personality tipping the scales. It's been shown that a family history of substance abuse, depression or manic depression increases the risk for eating disorders. And in terms of personality, many anorexics are described as perfectionist, overachieving types—"good" children who never rebelled; while about one-third of bulimics have addictive personalities and struggle with drug or alcohol abuse as well. One conclusion seems clear:

Eating disorders are complex problems that demand a sensitive, multi-dimensional approach. "For me, this is one of the more challenging fields in psychiatry," says Dr. Patel. Her commitment to patients is apparent in their enthusiastic response to the program. Laura, who graduated after seven weeks in the program last fall, credits it with providing important self-insights and newfound inner strength, as well as helping shed the behaviors that characterized her condition.

What to Do if Someone You Know Needs Help. If you believe someone you care about has an eating disorder, say something. That's the advice of Jennifer (not her real name), 20, another recent graduate of the eating disorders unit at Christ Hospital and Medical Center. Like so many people with eating disorders, Jennifer disguised her problem from her family. Her high school friends suspected it, however, and told a school counselor, who talked to Jennifer and provided information about the disorder's dangers. But Jennifer continued to eat only minimal amounts of food and then purge through vomiting and using up to 30 laxatives a day. Starved of nutrition and suffering from severe electrolyte imbalances, she began experiencing blackouts. Finally, her friends gave her an ultimatum: "Tell your parents or we will." "I didn't want my mom and dad to hear it from someone else, so one night I told them," she says. The next day her mother investigated treatment programs and checked Jennifer into Christ Hospital and Medical Center.

Recovery has been a difficult process. The first time Jennifer was hospitalized, she was so malnourished she required intravenous nutrition. One day she tore out the IVs in anger and needed a feeding tube installed for about a week. Discharged six weeks later, Jennifer resumed her self-destructive ritual within days. So she was hospitalized again for almost eight weeks in the spring of 1989.

Her relapse was not unusual. More than 30 percent of the people who seek treatment for eating disorders need follow-up care. The second time, however, everything clicked for Jennifer. "It was hard for me to let go of the idea that I could achieve happiness only through thinness. I always felt enormously fat, even at 5'5", 110 pounds. But thanks to the staff at Christ Hospital and Medical Center I realize I don't want to go through life obsessed with weight and afraid of food."

To join an eating disorders support group near you, call the National Association of Anorexia Nervosa and Associated Disorders at 708-831-3438. For more information on eating disorders and treatment options, call Christ Hospital and Medical Center at 708-857-4242. For referral to a quality therapist, call 1-800-347-COPE.

Articles in this issue written by Cindy Rippo, a Chicago-area freelance writer.

Laura hid her binging and purging incredibly well. It was a secret she shared with no one. "Even my ex-husband didn't know for eight of the nine years of our marriage," she says.

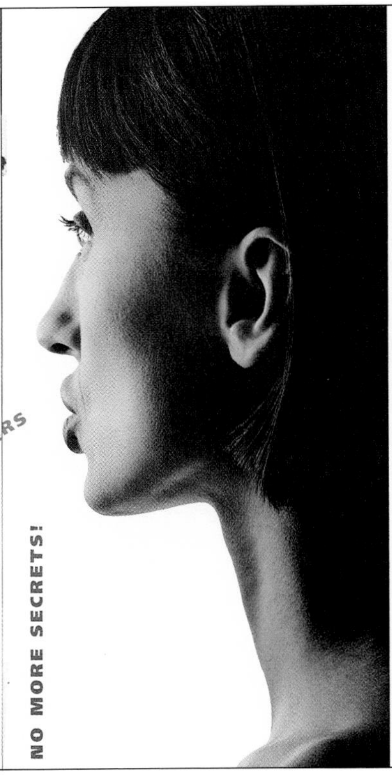

NO MORE SECRETS!

WHEN THIN CAN DO YOU IN–

EATING DISORDERS FACTS

What It Is: There are two major eating disorders: Anorexia nervosa (self-starvation) and bulimia nervosa (binging and purging). Many victims exhibit aspects of both problems. It's estimated that about half of anorexics eventually become bulimic when fasting becomes too dangerous.

Who Gets It: The majority (90 percent to 95 percent) are women, although the number of men may be on the rise. Most victims develop it some time between the preteen years and early adulthood.

Warning Signals: Often an eating disorder is preceded by a diet or rapid weight loss. Not all of the following symptoms are present in all victims. • Intense interest in food. May prepare elaborate meals for others, seek jobs in grocery stores or restaurants, hoard or steal food. • Obsessive fear of weight gain. Spends inordinate time thinking and talking about ways of becoming or staying thin. • Excessive weight loss, especially with anorexics. Bulimics' weight can vary from underweight to overweight. • Distorted body image. Even when average or underweight, victim feels fat or that body parts are fat. • Refusal to gain weight even when underweight. • Binging—secretly consuming large quantities of food, with a feeling of being out of control. An average of two or more binges a week for at least three months is typical. • Purging by means of self-induced vomiting or using laxatives, diuretics or emetics. • Hypergymnasia, or controlling weight gain through excessive self-punishing bouts of exercise. • Denial that a problem exists.

AWARENESS WINTER 1990 3

3.

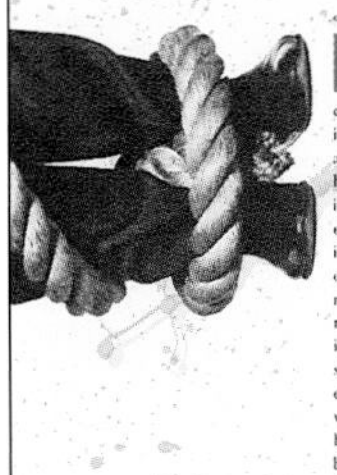

CONTINUED FROM COVER

Scientists have told us that the fear/stress/anxiety response is a survival instinct rooted deep in our brain, part of our evolutionary baggage. When a human's "survival" is threatened, our body releases a rush of adrenalin enabling us to fight or flee. Except today, humankind's survival is not dependent on escaping hungry animals (even though physiologically our bodies still respond as if it did). Our survival instincts kick in during a tough day at work, driving on the expressway, arguing with a spouse and other modern-day stressors. • Our physiological response, however, is not that different than it was in prehistoric days. Medical science has known since the 1920s that when an organism is frightened or otherwise stressed, the brain responds by activating the sympathetic nervous system. The heartbeat speeds up and breathing quickens to maximize blood and oxygen capacity. Blood is shunted away from the skin and internal organs to reduce the possibility of damage from a wound. Instead it moves to the muscles in preparation for action. At the same time, the liver releases glucose, the pancreas rushes insulin, the adrenal cortex churns out cortisol (adrenalin) and the thyroid outputs thyroid hormones. Fueled by this potent mix, the organism assesses the seriousness of the threat and either enters the fray or runs. • Scientists also attribute our anxiety to humans' larger brains, which contain a built-in level of stress found in no other species. We have "a continuously buzzing dissatisfaction [and] anxiety…that goes beyond what we need [for survival]" as one anthropologist describes it. On the one hand, this constant bee in the bonnet drives human beings to set high goals, work hard, and achieve them. On the other hand, it makes us unnecessarily sensitive to stresses both real and perceived. It also leads us to what psychologists call negative chain-link thinking or "catastrophizing." • But how much anxiety is too much? When should you seek help? • Here are some basic guidelines: **1.** If the severity of your symptoms is impairing your ability to drive, sleep, work, play, enjoy your relationships or otherwise function as you normally would, seek help. **2.** If you're managing to function normally, but anxious feelings have been bothering you for six months or more, seek help. **3.** If, for six months or more, you've suffered physical complaints for which your physician can't find a cause, seek help. **4.** If you don't fit any of the above categories, but you feel you want help or need help, seek help. • Where do you get help? Christ Hospital and Medical Center offers a comprehensive array of mental health services, including seminars on mental health issues and care for anxiety disorders. If you would like more information about these services, call 857-4242. • Christ Hospital and Medical Center also offers a support group, Emotions Anonymous, for those dealing with emotional problems, stress and lifestyle changes. It meets every Friday from 7:30 p.m. to 9:30 p.m. in the hospital's Harbor Room free of charge. For information call 383-0200. • **The Big 7 Anxiety Disorders—Can You Identify Them?** Psychiatrists agree there are seven major classifications of anxiety disorders, according to Robert G. Zadylak, M.D., Christ Hospital and Medical Center's chairperson and medical director of psychiatry. However, he says, "There are no sharp borders where one ends and another begins." For example, patients may have symptoms of more than one anxiety disorder at a time. Or, they'll experience anxiety in addition to another mental health problem, such as drug or alcohol abuse, or depression. Some may experience one anxiety disorder now and another disorder later in life. Here are the generally recognized classifications: **Panic Disorder.** An estimated 1.2 million people experience these sudden attacks of intense fear, accompanied by the physical symptoms of anxiety, in which the person feels he or she may lose control, "go crazy" or die. First attacks often occur with no apparent trigger. • **Agoraphobia.** Fear of panicking in public places where escape might be difficult or embarrassing, or where help might not be available. Often the individual with agoraphobia began by having panic attacks. As a result, the person avoids the places where panic might occur such as stores, parks, theaters or streets. Or else the person needs a companion when away from "safe" places (where no panic attacks have occurred) such as home. • **Social Phobia.** Fear and avoidance of social situations in which the person may be embarrassed or humiliated. Examples are fear of public speaking, writing or performing, fear of using public restrooms or fear of eating in public. • **Simple Phobia.** Fear and avoidance of a specific thing, place or situation that doesn't fall under agoraphobia or social phobia. Examples include fear of insects or animals, going to the dentist, airplane trips or driving on the expressway. Many simple phobias don't require treatment because the person can avoid the source of fear without it significantly impacting on his or her normal activities. Approximately 5 percent to 12 percent of Americans have simple phobic disorders in any six-month period. • **Obsessive-Compulsive Disorder.** Repetitive, unwanted thoughts or fear of something terrible happening unless the person performs certain repetitive, often senseless, rituals. For example, a woman may feel her house will burn down if she fails to surround the stovetop with buckets of water arranged in a perfect half circle before she leaves the house. If the ritual isn't performed exactly according to the "rules" the person has made up, he or she feels compelled to do it over and over again until it is "right." An estimated 2.4 million suffer from this form of anxiety. • **Post-Traumatic Stress Disorder.** This may occur in people who have experienced a terrible event such as an accident, a robbery, war or child abuse. Symptoms include re-experiencing the traumatic event and a feeling of emotional numbness or dissociation with the external world. Depression often accompanies. • **Generalized Anxiety Disorder.** Persistent, painful fear and worry, of at least six months duration, about two or more life circumstances. For example, anxiousness over losing one's job, combined with worry about an aging parent or a child who's not doing well in school, can raise a person's anxiety to an uncomfortable if not unbearable level. Normal functioning becomes difficult and several unpleasant physical and mental symptoms occur (see "Body Signs of Stress" and "Mind Signs of Stress" sidebars).

BODY SIGNS OF STRESS

Physical symptoms include: Clenched jaw, grinding teeth, wobbly legs, buzzing in the ears, blurry vision, hot or cold flashes, feelings of weakness, sweating, itching, heart palpitations, chest pain, throbbing pulse, fainting, choking feeling, shortness of breath, difficulty swallowing, lump in throat, gas, stomach pain, nausea, diarrhea, constipation, vomiting, urge to urinate, loss of sex drive, dry mouth, flushed or pale face, headaches, absence of menstrual period, rashes, cold sores, acne break outs. Before attributing physical symptoms to anxiety, it's important to have a medical evaluation. That's why your personal physician will screen for other diseases or illnesses before referring you to a mental health professional.

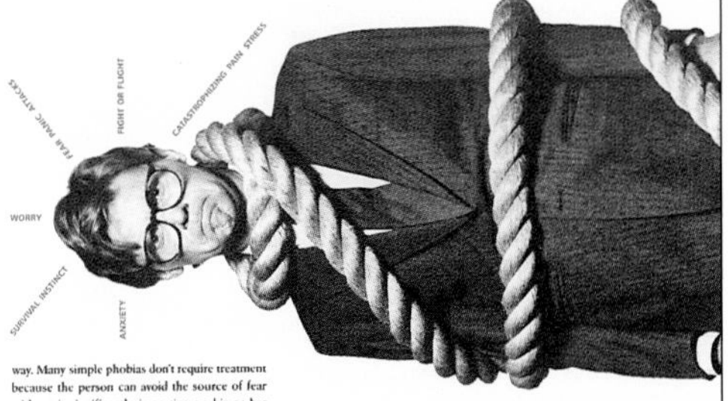

MIND SIGNS OF STRESS

In addition to the physical symptoms of stress and the symptoms listed under "The Big 7 Disorders," anxiety may cause you to feel: Hazy, foggy, dazed, as though the environment seems distant or unreal. Confused. Forgetful. Spaced out. Difficulty in concentrating. Absent-minded, tense, jittery, wound up, shaky, panicky, hyperaware of everything around you, supersensitive and self conscious. Constantly scanning the room with your eyes. Jumpy, irritable, angry. Worried and fearful. Afraid of being humiliated, of seeming crazy, of losing control, of physical injury or death, of losing your mind. If these symptoms persist, you may want to contact a mental health professional.

AWARENESS FALL 1989 3

4.

Covers (1,2,3) and spreads (4,5) from recruitment publication for college students.

DESIGN FIRM: Graphica, Inc., Miamisburg, Ohio

ART DIRECTOR/ DESIGNER: Cindy Schnell

ILLUSTRATORS: Kevin Burke, Jeff Stapleton, Mike Bonilla, Cindy Schnell

1.

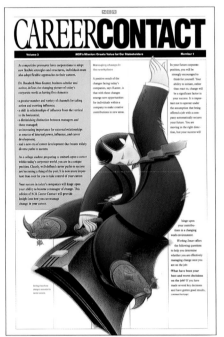

2.

3.

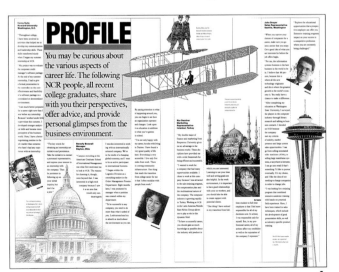

4.

5.

Pharmaceutical research

Cover (1) and spread (2)

from an in-house

employee publication.

DESIGNER: Holly Russell/

Glaxo, Inc., Research

Triangle Park, North

Carolina

ILLUSTRATOR:

Anthony Russo

WRITERS: Geraldine

Duncan, Rick Sluder,

Cindy Schroeder

1.

SPINACH AND BROWN RICE CASSEROLE

1 T. polyunsaturated oil
1 large onion, chopped
2 c. mushrooms, sliced
1 clove garlic
1 egg white
1 T. whole wheat flour
2 c. low-fat cottage cheese
10 ounces frozen chopped spinach, drained
3 c. cooked brown rice
Freshly ground black pepper
½ t. thyme
2 T. Parmesan cheese
2 T. sunflower seeds

Heat oil in a Dutch oven and saute onion, mushrooms and garlic until tender. In a small bowl, mix egg white, flour and cottage cheese. Add to sauteed vegetables along with spinach. Stir in rice, pepper, thyme and 1 tablespoon of Parmesan cheese.

Turn into a 12-by-8-inch baking dish prepared with non-stick spray, and top with remaining cheese and sunflower seeds. Bake at 375 degrees for at least 30 minutes. 8 servings.

Source: The American Heart Association Cookbook

into solid fat (bad) by saturation.

Important CF Tip No. 3: Learn nutrition label-ese, and don't be taken in.

So I vowed to absorb all this low-cholesterol wisdom and avoid this food or increase that one. But then it would fall to my wife to adapt the menus. (Don't start. I know this is the '80s, I know I should do my share in the kitchen, I know that marriage is a partnership, I know, I know. But I don't cook, and I really don't want to talk about it.)

This situation led to some interesting discussions as dinner bubbled away. "Did you just glop some butter in the peas?" "Margarine." "That high-fat stuff you insist on buying?" "The stuff you bought won't melt." "Won't melt? Did you turn the burner on? Whaddyamean, won't melt?" Thus was born important CF Tip No. 4: When a cook you're married to suddenly clams up, grabs a knife and starts chopping carrots, back off.

Days pass, and we make a pleasant discovery. This lighter, lower-fat food is not bad. It's better than not bad. It's pretty good.

The American Heart Association Cookbook, which for reasons I can't remember we owned before this episode began, becomes our bible. Spinach and brown rice casserole. Chicken with broccoli-mushroom sauce. Curried butternut squash soup. All winners. We're excited. We talk about all the new tastes we've found, about all the new tastes we'll try.

We're feeling pretty good about ourselves. Until our 9-year-old finally tires of pushing the lemon marmalade chicken around the plate. "Mom," she says, "When are we going to have hot dogs again?"

The next weekend we go to a pizza place. They eat cheese-stuffed pasta. I have spaghetti with tomato sauce. Important CF Tip No. 5: Don't inflict your diet on those around you, no matter how right you are about the margarine.

I turn my exercising up a notch. Now I run at least five mornings a week, 20 to 60 minutes an outing. It feels good. It also raises my HDL, the experts say. HDL? Remember LDL? HDL is the other side of the coin, the high-density lipoprotein that may actually decrease the adherence of cholesterol to arterial walls.

My weight drops, which I don't need. At over 6 feet, I'm already about 160, 170 pounds. The diet slices 10 or 12 pounds more pounds before I know it.

I counter by eating more snacks. When I get home, I no longer pop a beer and grab a handful of peanuts: I pop a beer and grab a couple of zero-fat hard pretzels—and sometimes pop another beer. I eat raisins and other dried fruit for the low-fat calories. I discover a new snack delicacy: peanut butter and raisins on a rice cracker.

Regardless, the weight keeps dropping, an aggravation I decide I'll just have to put up with. I've lost weight through exercise before, and it always levels off. I'm not going to quit dieting or exercising.

One morning I'm out before sun-up. Something catches my eye on the horizon. I look up and see what must be the end of a meteor shower: two or three shooting stars in quick succession.

Hmmm, I think. This cholesterol fighting's not so bad.

Sometimes, though, this cholesterol fighting's awfully frustrating. Especially when you have to fend off comments from well-meaning friends, including those at the office.

"You're losing too much weight," one co-worker says. "You look sick. People are beginning to talk."

I feel great, I think. I really do.

"Stick to your diet, just loosen up," says another. "Don't be so strict. All things in moderation, you know."

Right, I think. I should aim for a moderate heart attack.

I make up my mind not to talk about my diet, but I fail. Things slip out. Friends ask questions. I answer. They begin their subtle badgering. I realize this is their perverse way of showing they're rooting for me.

I appreciate it.

Three months since the 228 reading. It's February, and I'm ready to be tested again. I tell my wife that this has really been easy. I don't feel like I've been on a diet. I haven't been hungry. I've enjoyed my food. Easy. A few rocky stretches, but in general, easy.

In fact, I realize it has been no simple matter at all. It has required—not sacrifices, really—but a willingness to change, to try new food combinations, to pass up the ice cream. It has also required a ton of support from many different people, but mainly my wife.

I have the test. The next day, heart in throat, I call occupational health services. This is silly, I tell my heart. Get back down there where you belong. After all I've done for you, you could at least do this for me. My heart ignores me.

The health services people offer pleasantries and say some other stuff I don't remember. I recall hearing only one thing: 177.

177. As in under 200. A 22 percent drop in three months. There are a few numbers I'll remember the rest of my life: my draft lottery number in 1972, my wife and daughter's birth date, and 177.

Some things in life you can control.

That night our family goes back to the pizza place, and we order the real thing. One honest-to-goodness, cheese-drenched pizza. Hold the soybeans.

If you're curious about your cholesterol level, occupational health services offers a free screening for full-time employees. If it's high, they also offer counseling, printed information and tips on how to lower it. Call ext. 2465 for a screening appointment.

2.

Cover (1), spreads
(2,3,4,5), and spot
illustration (6) from
house magazine.
DESIGN FIRM: Cook and
Shanosky, Princeton,
New Jersey
ART DIRECTORS/
DESIGNERS: Roger Cook,
Don Shanosky
DESIGNER:
Cathryn Cook
COVER ART:
Charles Ross (1)
PHOTOGRAPHERS:
Charlotte Raymond (3),
Ken Knott (5)

Squibb

Medical/pharmaceutical

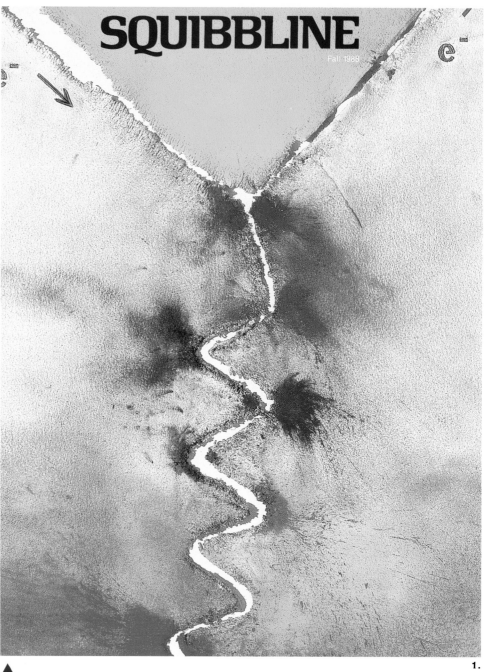

SQUIBBLINE

Fall 1988

1.

P P & T

Visitors from BASF

Post-Squibb

New Los Angeles Distribution Center Dedicated

2.

PREVENTIVE CARDIOLOGY

3.

OSKAR PAUL WINTERSTEINER, Ph.D.,
AND HIS 27 YEARS AT SQUIBB By Elizabeth Zee

EARLY YEARS IN AMERICA

4.

M E E T I N G   R E P O R T

ITALY

Expanding profile of aztreonam

5.

?   **?**   **?**   **?**

6.

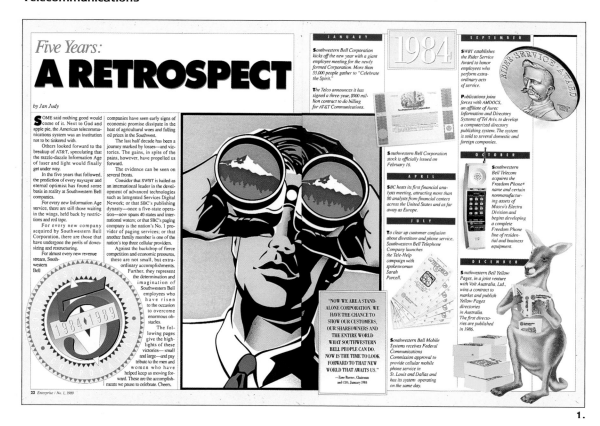

1.

2.

Cover (3) and spreads
(1,2) from issue of in-
house quarterly
publication; spot
illustration (4) and cover
(5) from other issues.
DESIGN FIRM:
Hawthorne/Wolfe, Inc.,
St. Louis, Missouri
ART DIRECTOR:
John Howze
ILLUSTRATORS: Chris
Gall (2), Rene Milot (3)

3.

4.

5.

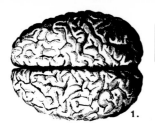

1.

Partnership for Neighborhood Development, Richard St. John, executive director of OPDC, and Lynn Portnoff of the Local 4 Block Club – three leading community representatives.

Ms. Phillips has been a neighborhood advocate in Oakland since 1973, and was executive director of OPDC.

Mr. St. John, previously her assistant, replaced Ms. Phillips as OPDC executive director when she recently assumed a new citywide role with the Pittsburgh Partnership for Neighborhood Development.

Mr. Forsythe says, "These community leaders have consistently given us a candid grass roots measure of our impact in the surrounding neighborhood. That kind of input is essential if we are to be a good neighbor in our immediate environment."

Mr. Forsythe has met frequently with community representatives who were concerned about traffic and congestion in the neighborhood. Those meetings have resulted in creation of an off-site parking and shuttle system for medical center employees that has taken approximately 1,000 vehicles a day out of the Oakland parking scene. **T**he MHCD also instituted valet parking service for patients and visitors to help minimize traffic tie-ups near the

hospitals, move cars into parking garages, and get drivers and passengers to their destinations in the medical center.

Additionally, construction is under way on a nearby 1,168-space parking garage-sports complex that will take more medical center people out of the on-campus commercial parking system and free those spaces for other commuters and visitors.

"**C**learly," Mr. Forsythe adds, "the community feels an enormous impact from both the daily operations of the medical center and the Partnership building program. To get the neighborhood more directly involved in our operations, the MHCD and OPDC are cooperating in Job Links. This is a program that encourages local organizations to identify and help prepare residents for employment at our institutions.

"**S**ome of those jobs result from the increasing scope of activities at the institutions. Others result when our current people advance their careers by taking advantage of our employee educational programs. One such program is Project Presby Partners, which helps participating employees get college degrees."

Mr. Forsythe says even the basic premise for the Partnership construction project evolved in community

planning sessions. "We had to address community concerns that our growth would jeopardize existing residential and open spaces. MHCD representatives assured the community that there would be no encroachment into residential neighborhoods as a part of the Partnership construction.

"**T**he turning point came when we announced, 'we're going to go up.' We decided that everybody's interests would best be served by adopting what is called an 'air rights' plan. This means all new construction is being built above existing structures.

"**I**n the case of the Presbyterian-University Hospital Tower, that means adding a 16-level center wing in front of an existing 13-level structure. All of this is happening while the Hospital maintains its busy pace of daily activities."

Despite the size and complexity of the medical center's operation and growth, Presbyterian-University Hospital's mission remains relatively simple. M. Patricia Shehorn, administrator of the Hospital, and MHCD vice president, Clinical Administration, concludes: "We measure our academic and research accomplishments nationally; we weigh our impact on the economy of the region; and we recognize that we are an everpresent factor in the life of Oakland. Still, the most important measure of our impact is taken one patient at a time."

2.

Spread (2), covers (3,4) and spot illustrations/ photos (1,5) from magazine directed at the corporate community and the health care industry.

DESIGN FIRM:

Landesberg Design Associates, Pittsburgh, Pennsylvania

DESIGNER:

Rick Landesberg

PHOTOGRAPHER:

Bill Redic (4)

ILLUSTRATOR: Joe Ciardiello (1,3)

TOWER

Presbyterian-
University
Hospital
of Pittsburgh
Medical and
Health Care Division
University of
Pittsburgh

Volume 2, Number 1
Summer 1989

The academic
medical center:
affecting
countless lives—
around the
world and
around the
corner

3.

TOWER

Presbyterian-
University
Hospital
of Pittsburgh

Affiliate,
Medical and
Health Care Division
University of
Pittsburgh

Volume 1, Number 2
Annual Report Issue
Winter 1988/1989

The
centuries-old
quest for the
answer to the
more than
200 diseases
called
cancer.

81.—COMMON CELANDINE.
CHELIDONIUM MAJUS.

*An 18th century cure for
cancer consisting of garden
sorrel, celandine, and the
inner bark from the south
side of a persimmon tree.*

4.

5.

155

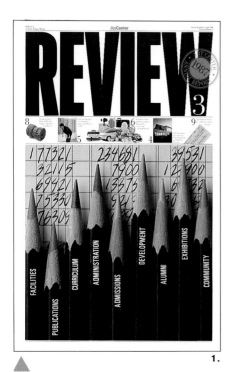

1.

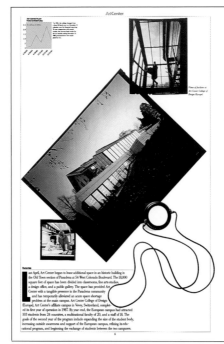

2.

Covers (1,4,6), spreads (2,5,7) and photo (3) from alumni and student newsletter.

DESIGN FIRM: Pentagram, San Francisco, California

ART DIRECTOR/ DESIGNER: Kit Hinrichs

DESIGNERS: Terri Driscoll, Karen Boone (1), Lenore Bartz (6)

ILLUSTRATOR: Douglas Boyd (2)

PHOTOGRAPHERS: Steven A. Heller (1,4,6), Barry Robinson (2)

3.

4.

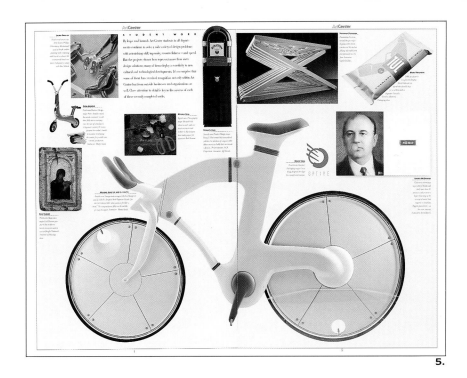

5.

6.

7.

Art Center College of Design

Design school

Cover (1) and interior (2) of promotional folder mailed to industry professionals to generate interest in a forthcoming conference.

DESIGN FIRM: Clement Mok designs, San Francisco, California

ART DIRECTOR: Clement Mok

DESIGNERS: Charles Routhier, Lori Nason, Sandra Koenig

ILLUSTRATOR: Mike Wiggins

1.

Apple Computer
Computer hardware and software

2.

1.

Jerry Lieberman Productions, Inc.

Animation

2.

Cover (1), pages (2) and illustration (3) from promotional flip book.

DESIGN FIRM:

The Pushpin Group, New York, New York

ART DIRECTOR/

ILLUSTRATOR:

Seymour Chwast

3.

1.

Promotional campaign to revamp company image, which was becoming overly identified with just one paper in its line. Shown are cover (1) of large sheet swatchbook; sleeve and covers (2), and spreads (3,4) from smaller swatchbooks which describe Niles, Michigan, where the mill is located.

DESIGN FIRM: The Duffy Design Group, Minneapolis, Minnesota
DESIGNER/ILLUSTRATOR: Charles S. Anderson
ILLUSTRATOR: Lynn Shulte

Champion Imagination 26

1.

Cover (1) and interior (2) of promotional book focusing on "white"; spreads (3) from brochure found inside book.

DESIGN FIRM: Janet Odgis & Company, Inc., New York, New York

ART DIRECTOR/ DESIGNER: Janet Odgis

DESIGNERS: Elizabeth Bakacs, Richard Manville

New Champion Kromekote 2000

white on white

Imagination 26

2.

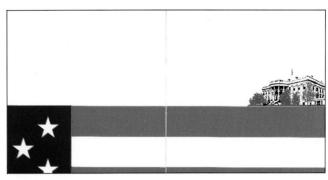

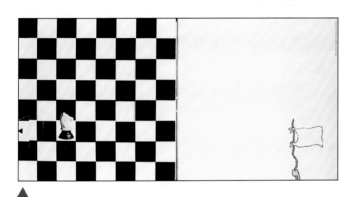

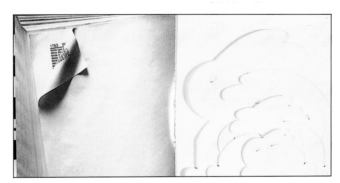

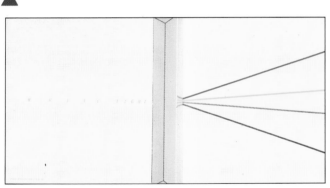

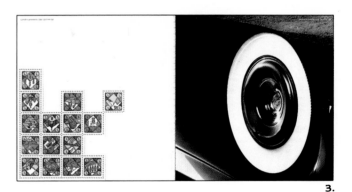

3.

1.

Covers (1), spreads (2,3,4,5,6) and illustration (7) from series of promotional brochures each telling the story of an American centennarian.

DESIGNER/COPYWRITER:

Richard Hess

PHOTOGRAPHER:

Dmitri Kasterine

(contemporary images)

COPYWRITER:

Jo Durden-Smith

2.

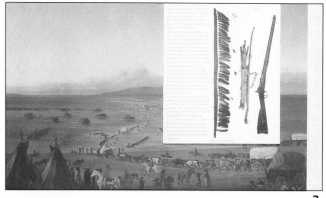

3.

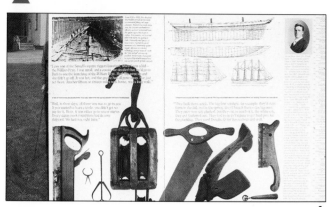

4.

5.

6.

7.

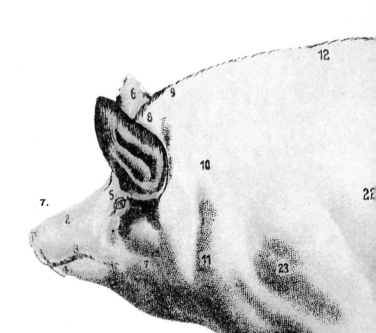

The late night phone calls
Du Pont loves to get.

1.

It's three in the morning, and you've been working straight through the night. Things are running smoothly. But suddenly, you remember …you've forgotten something!…there was something you planned on doing yesterday…what was it? Oh, yeah! Now you remember. You were going to order more intermediate materials from Du Pont. But now look…3 AM!! Well, what are you waiting for? Go ahead, make our night. Call us! And so it goes. Smoothly. With Du Pont's new 24-hour toll-free number.

Now, you can call on Du Pont day or night.

Why is Du Pont introducing a 24-hour number? Why should we go to the trouble? Trouble?!! When it comes to serving you—our valued customer—nothing, not even staying awake all night, is too much trouble.

What our number's for…

There are plenty of reasons, in fact, for us to offer a 24-hour number for our polymer and chemical specialty intermediates. How else can you place orders or request product samples after 5 PM Eastern time? (This is especially important for those of you located west of the Mississippi.) How else can we help you with last-minute order changes or get your shipment status? How can we respond to your needs when you're running day and night, if we're not? You could say, Du Pont never sleeps. And the truth is, now we don't.

…and what it's not for.

At our end of the line, you'll find specially trained Du Pont technicians. And though they can't provide pricing information or take the place of your customer sales representative, they'll be there to put you in touch with the right person just as quickly as possible.

You'll never lose our number if you stick it on your phone.

Put our sticker on your phone. That way you'll be able to find us whenever you need us—24 hours a day.

For polymer and chemical
specialty intermediates
1-800-231-0998
Du Pont Never Sleeps

2.

Whenever you're
at the end of your line…
call Du Pont.

3.

That's right. Du Pont now has our own 24-hour, toll-free number staffed by our specially trained technicians (not an answering service). So call us—night or day—when you need us. Whether you're depleting your Du Pont supplies faster than expected. Or you want to initiate order-tracking for a shipment due for arrival. Or you need to modify an order. Or you just want to ask us a question. You can even phone us at four in the morning to request a product sample. Here's how it works: Our after-hours technicians are specially trained to handle all your calls—including emergencies. Depending on the urgency of your call, they'll process your request on the spot, coordinate an action for first thing the following morning, or, if necessary, contact the person you need then and there. They are your 24-hour link to the full range Du Pont resources.

A true story.

'Twas literally the night before Christmas when all through a California manufacturer's plant almost nothing was stirring, for they were running out of an important Du Pont product. They reached our late-night technician located in Victoria, Texas who immediately contacted the East Coast manager who was on call that night. She, in turn, returned the call to California within 15 minutes, informing them that the very individual they needed to speak to would get back to them in less than an hour. And he did. Arrangements for more material were made and the plant, it can be said, manufactured happily ever after. Now, if our new 24-hour line can operate this efficiently on Christmas Eve, just think what we can do for you on the other 364 days in the year.

You'll never lose our number if you stick it on your phone.

Put our sticker on your phone. That way you'll be able to find us whenever you need us—24 hours a day.

For polymer and chemical
specialty intermediates
1-800-231-0998
Du Pont Never Sleeps

4.

Du Pont

Chemicals

Covers (1,3) and spreads (2,4) from pieces in a 3-part direct-mail campaign announcing and promoting a 24-hour toll-free service hotline.

AGENCY: Janet Hughes and Associates, Wilmington, Delaware

ART DIRECTOR: Donna Perzel

COPYWRITER: Richard Bieber-Scheidner

ILLUSTRATOR: Elwood Smith

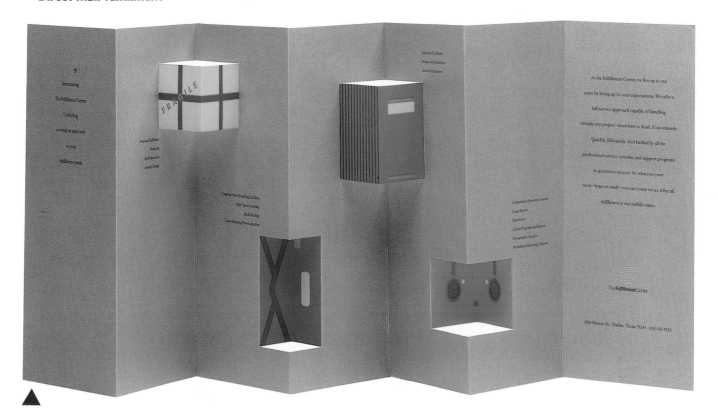

Opening announcement
and mini-capabilities
promotional foldout.
DESIGN FIRM: Sibley/
Peteet Design, Dallas,
Texas
DESIGNER: Judy Dolim
COPYWRITER:
Don Sibley

1.

AMERICAS TOWER

Since the first high rise office building was built in the late nineteenth century, the skyscraper has been an evolving art form. The construction of the classical skyscrapers of the 1920's and 30's introduced a new variation on the American commercial style that some say has rarely been equalled. Their loftiness of scale, distinctive classical features, and lavish use of ornamentation became symbolic of a city and a skyline familiar the world over. Theatrical, accessible, at times even excessive, they are skyscrapers whose primary effect is to delight.

After years of neutral International Style glass boxes, today's builders are once again humanizing the workplace with architecture that is practical, efficient and very appealing, with its use of color, ornament and down to earth textural effects. An excellent example of this new breed of office building can be found on the Avenue of the Americas between 45th and 46th streets. With its warm Finnish coral granite exteriors rising 50 stories to a striking ornamental top, its sweeping grand entrance, and adroit use of color, form and texture, Americas Tower is monumental opulence executed in very human terms—attractive, enticing, visually exciting.

2.

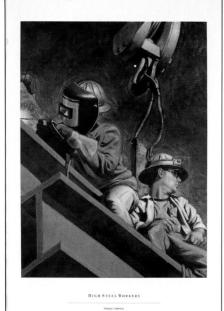

HIGH STEEL WORKERS

GEORGE CAMPBELL

3.

Americas Tower Partners

Commercial real estate

Cover (1) and art print (3) from foldout promotional piece for midtown Manhattan office tower; cover (2) of information insert from same brochure; cover (4), spreads (5,6) and spot diagrams (7,8) from hardcover promotional book in same campaign.

DESIGN FIRM: Lance Brown Design, Houston, Texas

ART DIRECTOR/ DESIGNER: Lance Brown

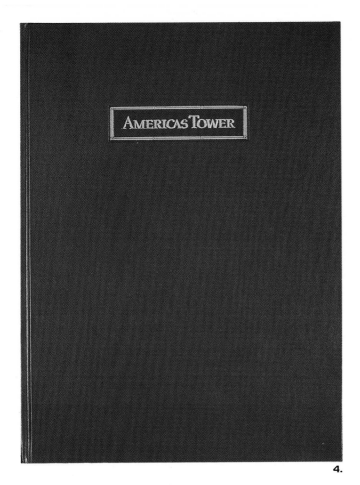

4.

In concept and context Americas Tower is a superb representative of the American commercial style. Designed by Swanke Hayden Connell Architects, the renowned architectural and interior design firm, Americas Tower is a seamless progression of color, texture, proportion and scale.

In appearance the tower seems to flow from the urban fabric that surrounds it, soaring 50-stories in a series of transitional setbacks to culminate in a lofty metal spire. Its frame is finished with gray glass windows alternating with stone cladding in the warm tones of Finnish coral granite, a color scheme that provides a harmonious counterpoint to the exterior of nearby Rockefeller Center. A stainless steel crest rising through the center of the facade emphasizes the building's verticality in a manner that relates Americas Tower to the city's preeminent architectural landmark, the Empire State Building.

With its masterful fusion of art and engineering, practicality and prestige, Americas Tower succeeds on a monumental scale as both a distinguished corporate environment and a superb artistic achievement. By day, with its ornamental metal top and polished granite detailing highlighted by the sun, the impression is one of undeniable style and stature. By night, as beacons of light play along the length of its elegant stone surface, Americas Tower projects a powerful and compelling new presence on Manhattan's skyline.

5.

6.

DESIGNER:

Kitte Pennace

ILLUSTRATOR:

George Campbell

COPYWRITERS:

Ann Kifer, Jolynn Rogers

PHOTOGRAPHER:

Tom Payne

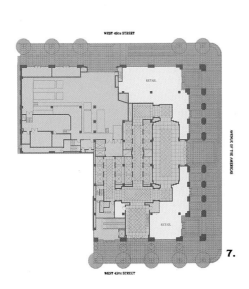

7.

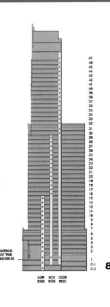

8.

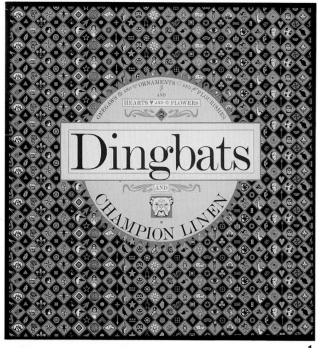

1.

Annual promotional series using reference material to encourage designers to keep paper samples. Shown are: cover (1) and interior (2) of folder containing various paper samples; spread (3) and covers (4) from samples; covers (5,6), samples (7) and spot illustrations (8) from additional promotions in series. DESIGN FIRM: Koppel & Scher, New York, New York
DESIGNER: Paula Scher

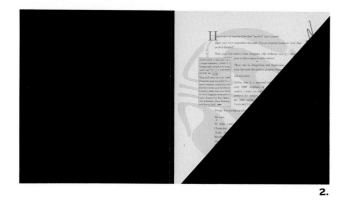

2.

3.

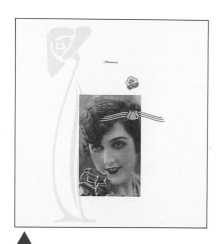

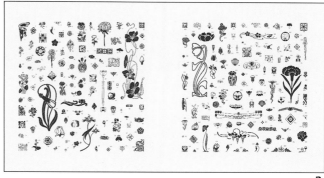

4.

Champion International

Paper products

5.

6.

7.

8.

TRIPLE CONDENSED GOTHIC   SHRIFTEN LIGHT   ZIERSCRIFT

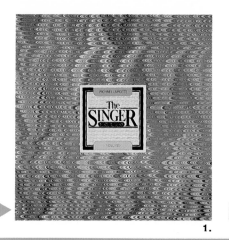

1.

2.

3.

Singer Printing

Printing

Promotional campaign using a series of direct-mail folios each one featuring the work of a different artist. Shown are covers (1,2,3) of folios and an open folio with contents (4).

DESIGN FIRM: The Black Point Group, San Francisco, California

ART DIRECTOR: Gary Priester

PHOTOGRAPHERS: Victor Budnik (2), Larry Keenan (3)

ILLUSTRATOR: Barbara Banthien (folio shown)

ARTIST: Peggy Skycraft (1)

COPYWRITER: Mary E. Carter

4.

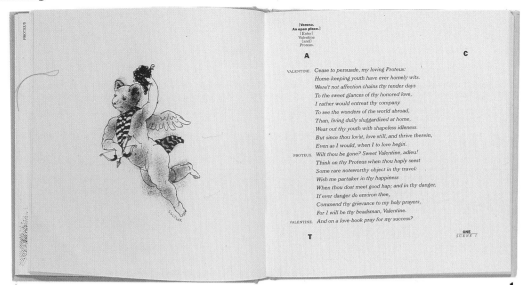

1.

Joint promotional edition of Shakespeare's "Two Gentlemen of Verona." Shown are spreads (1,2) and book with sleeve (3). Every year a different Shakespeare play gets this treatment.

DESIGNER: Martin Solomon/Royal Composing Room

ILLUSTRATOR: Isadore Seltzer

2.

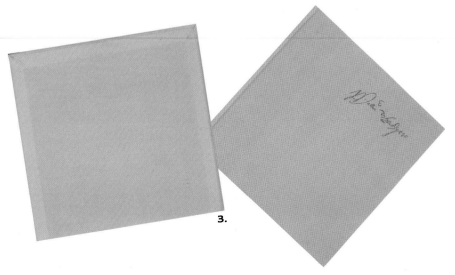

3.

Paper products

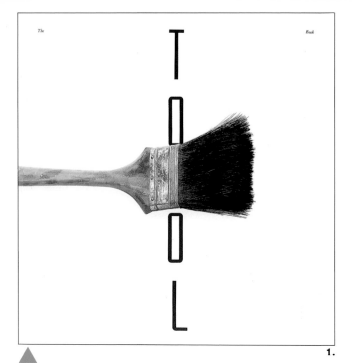

The **TOOL** *Book*

1.

2.

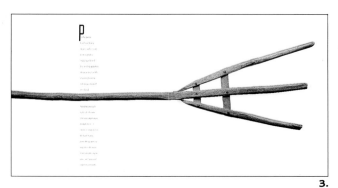

3.

Promotional series using ordinary objects to express individuality of "signatures." Shown are covers (1,2,5) and spreads (3,4,6,7,8,9) from three books in series.
DESIGN FIRM: Van Dyke Company, Seattle, Washington
DESIGNER: John Van Dyke
PHOTOGRAPHER: Terry Heffernan
COPYWRITER: Jon Bell

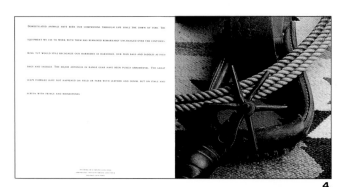

4.

Make Your Mark on Signature from Mead

5.

Signature in a bright white,
number-one coated paper
from Mead.
A glance reveals its superior qualities.
Its gloss finish,
as you can see from the cover,
provides you with dazzling dots
for crackling contrasts.
Its dull finish,
as you can see from this page,
has a combination
of low reflection and high resolution
that no other paper can match.

Classic from the ground up.

6.

Spit and polish.
Some shoes
earn their look
by enduring
digits
and oxygen.
Reads of mires
barks,
and brushable
angle kin
called pencil
and shine
as their feet.

7.

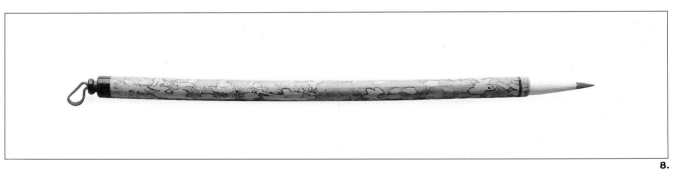

8.

Signature is beautiful from the inside out. From the beginning, we wanted Signature to be the best of its
kind. So we started at the beginning. With better pulp. New manufacturing processes. Even an
improved delivery and service system. The result? Signature is the new quality No. 1 coated grade.
Period.

9.

The **All-American Publication Papers** Book

Champion
Champion International Corporation

1.

Cover (1) and spread (2) from promotional sample book with pages cut in half to allow direct comparisons of different papers; cover (3), photograph (4) and spreads (5) from additional book in series.

DESIGN FIRM: Weisz Yang Dunkelberger, Westport, Connecticut

ART DIRECTORS/ DESIGNERS: Larry Yang, David Dunkelberger

DESIGNER:

Bernard Reynoso

ILLUSTRATOR:

Bob Giusti

PHOTOGRAPHERS:

Henry Wolf, William Hubbell, Amos Chan, Photo Researchers, Inc., Animals Animals, The Image Bank

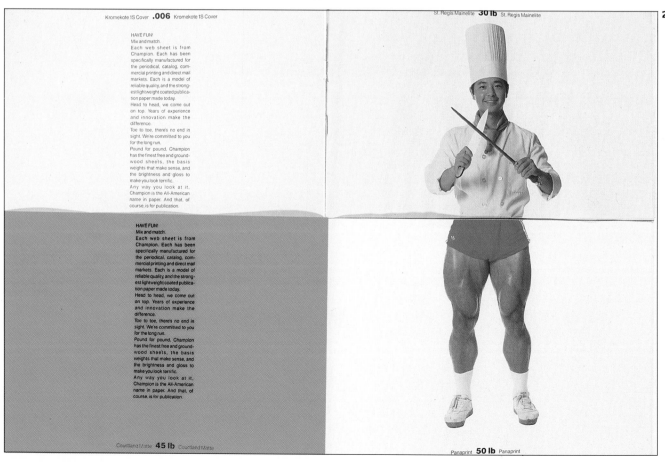

2.

4.

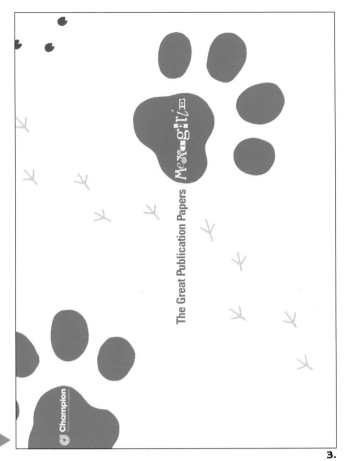

3.

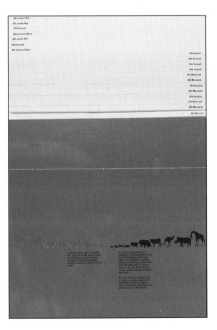

5.

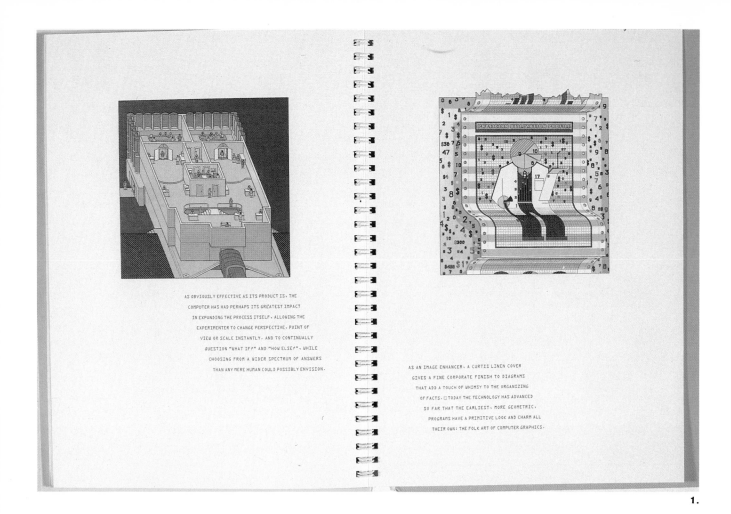

AS OBVIOUSLY EFFECTIVE AS ITS PRODUCT IS, THE
COMPUTER HAS HAD PERHAPS ITS GREATEST IMPACT
IN EXPANDING THE PROCESS ITSELF, ALLOWING THE
EXPERIMENTER TO CHANGE PERSPECTIVE, POINT OF
VIEW OR SCALE INSTANTLY, AND TO CONTINUALLY
QUESTION "WHAT IF?" AND "HOW ELSE?", WHILE
CHOOSING FROM A WIDER SPECTRUM OF ANSWERS
THAN ANY MERE HUMAN COULD POSSIBLY ENVISION.

AS AN IMAGE ENHANCER, A CURTIS LINEN COVER
GIVES A FINE CORPORATE FINISH TO DIAGRAMS
THAT ADD A TOUCH OF WHIMSY TO THE ORGANIZING
OF FACTS. □ TODAY THE TECHNOLOGY HAS ADVANCED
SO FAR THAT THE EARLIEST, MORE GEOMETRIC,
PROGRAMS HAVE A PRIMITIVE LOOK AND CHARM ALL
THEIR OWN: THE FOLK ART OF COMPUTER GRAPHICS.

1.

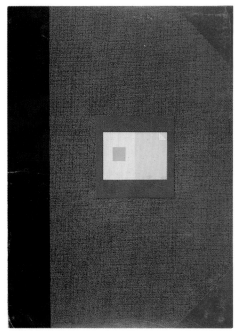

3.

James River
Paper products

Cover (3), spreads (1,2)
and spot illustration (4)
from brochure promoting
James River uncoated
papers to corporate
marketing and annual
report designers.
DESIGN FIRM: Sibley/
Peteet Design, Dallas,
Texas

2.

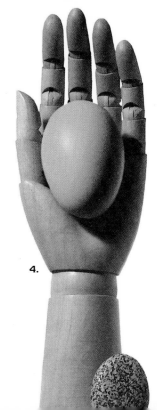

ART DIRECTOR/

DESIGNER/

COPYWRITER:

Rex Peteet

COPYWRITER:

Mary Keck

PHOTOGRAPHERS:

Richard Reens, Stewart

Charles Cohen, Elle

Schuster, Dan Nelken,

Ron Scott

ILLUSTRATORS: John
Craig, Stephen Alcorn,
Andrzej Dudzinski, Brad
Holland, James McMullan
& Sibley/Peteet Design
staff

4.

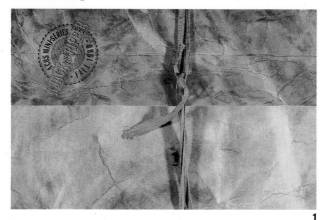

1

2.

Cover (1) and interior (2) of foldout piece, directed at media buyers, promoting "Jack the Ripper" mini-series as an investigative report rather than a thriller.

AGENCY: Backer Spielvogel Bates, New York, New York

ART DIRECTOR: Andrew Kner

ART DIRECTOR/ DESIGNER: Lynda Decker

PHOTOGRAPHER: Tony Generico

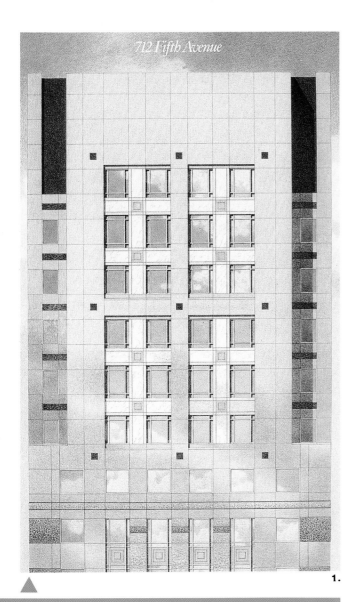

712 Fifth Avenue

1.

7

712 Fifth Avenue has been created to achieve a single purpose: to provide importance surroundings for distinguished office tenants.

What sets 712 Fifth Avenue apart? In a word, everything. From the unique blend of classic and 21st century architecture to its exclusive location and attention lavished on every detail, 712 Fifth Avenue embodies excellence. It is a milestone in the development of premier quality office buildings. A building as prestigious and influential as its tenants.

The graceful office tower, designed by the renowned architects Kohn Pedersen Fox Associates PC, is exceptional in every aspect of its creation. Its style, form and materials complement the surrounding architectural landscape. Three French neo-classical facades on Fifth Avenue have been meticulously restored to their turn-of-the-century splendor. Spectacular landmark windows, designed by the French artist René Lalique, have been restored to their pristine beauty and are a further reminder of the building's Fifth Avenue heritage.

The 53-story office tower soars dramatically above these treasures. The tower is sheathed in luminous grey limestone whose textured surfaces allow the natural play of light and shadow to define its contours. Lightly polished pearl-grey Mariposa marble, in a lustrous motif evocative of the Lalique windows below, is framed in limestone and accented with black Cambrian granite. Monumental four-square windows punctuated by glistening bronze medallions highlight the center of the tower.

712 Fifth Avenue reflects the caring eye of its owners. The finest building materials and construction standards, world-class amenities, state-of-the-art building technology, comprehensive safety and security systems, and flexible interior spaces unite to create the ultimate accommodations for the world's most discerning businesses.

2.

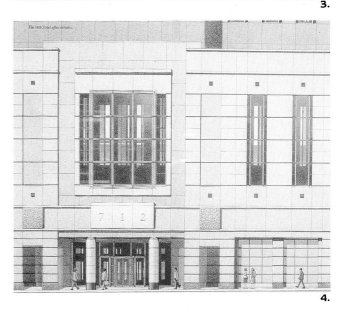

712 Fifth Avenue is a commanding presence in the Midtown skyline.

3.

The 38th Street office entrance.

7 1 2

4.

Solomon Equities

Commerical real estate

Cover (1) and spreads (2,3,4) from hardcover promotional book for 712 Fifth Avenue office building.

DESIGN FIRM: Vignelli Associates, New York, New York

ART DIRECTOR:

Massimo Vignelli

DESIGNERS: Michael Bierut, Michael Leone

ILLUSTRATOR:

Brian Burr

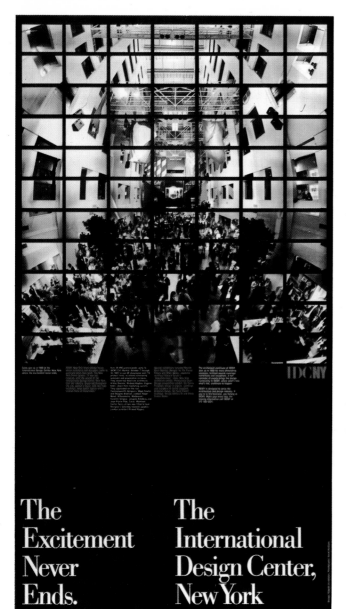

1.

2.

3.

4.

5.

6.

Cover (3) and spread (4) from promotional brochure announcing the availability of retail space—previously reserved exclusively for furniture companies—to design and architectural firms; promotional poster (1); covers (5,6), spread (2) and spot illustration (7) from bimonthly newsletter.

DESIGN FIRM: Vignelli Associates, New York, New York

ART DIRECTOR: Michael Bierut

DESIGNER: Lucy Cossentino

7.

1.

An American tradition, a true sports legacy, is entering a new era. And CBS is proud to carry on this grand tradition— Major League Baseball.

2.

3.

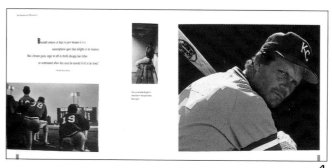

4.

5.

Sleeve (1) and spreads (3,4) from promotional book for baseball telecasts; cover (2) and spot illustration (5) from promotional folder directed at advertisers.

AGENCY: Backer Spielvogel Bates, New York, New York

ART DIRECTOR: Andrew Kner

ART DIRECTOR/ DESIGNER: Jim Shefcik

CBS

Broadcasting

1.

2.

3.

5.

Steelcase

Office interiors

Covers (2,3) and spreads
(4,5) from brochures
outlining sales incentive
program; cover of folder
(1) containing
brochures.

DESIGN FIRM: Williams
Marketing Services,
Grand Rapids, Michigan

**ART DIRECTOR/
DESIGNER:** Roger Snider
COPYWRITERS: Michael
Cox, John Crouse

Computer hardware and software

1.

2.

3.

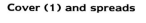

Cover (1) and spreads (2,3) from conference directory highlighting the theme "Seeing is Believing."

DESIGN FIRM: Tim Girvin Design, Inc., Seattle, Washington

CREATIVE DIRECTOR/ COPYWRITER: Tom Corddry

ART DIRECTOR/ ILLUSTRATOR: Tim Girvin

DESIGNER: Stephen Pannone, Kevin Henderson

ILLUSTRATOR: Anton Kimball

1.

2.

3.

4.

Cover (1) and spreads
(2,3,4) from direct-mail
promotional book.
DESIGN FIRM:
Charles S. Anderson
Design Co.
Minneapolis, Minnesota

ART DIRECTOR/
DESIGNER/
ILLUSTRATOR:
Charles S. Anderson
ILLUSTRATOR:
Lynn Schulte
COPYWRITER: Jarl Olson

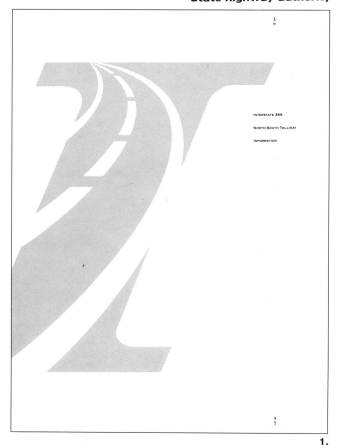

INTERSTATE 355

NORTH-SOUTH TOLLWAY

INFORMATION

1.

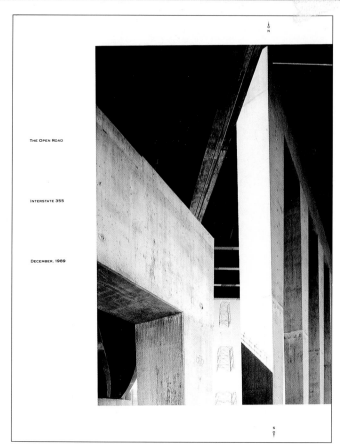

THE OPEN ROAD

INTERSTATE 355

DECEMBER, 1989

2.

Cover (2) and spreads
(3,4) from brochure
promoting the opening of
Interstate 355; cover of
press kit folder (1).
DESIGN FIRM: Vogele
Stoik Associates, Inc.,
Chicago, Illinois
ART DIRECTOR:
Ted Stoik
DESIGNER: Carol Dean
PHOTOGRAPHER: Tony
Armour, Chicago, Illinois

3.

T
HE OPEN ROAD IS A NATURAL

EXTENSION OF ITS HOME. IT IS

UNDERSTATED AS IT WINDS

BELOW GRADE THROUGH ITS

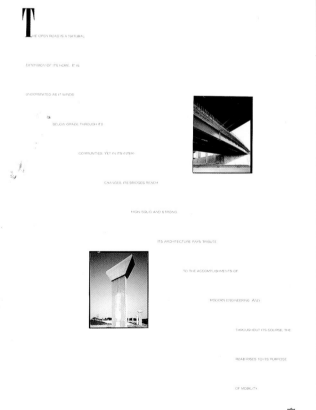

COMMUNITIES. YET IN ITS INTER-

CHANGES, ITS BRIDGES REACH

HIGH, SOLID AND STRONG.

ITS ARCHITECTURE PAYS TRIBUTE

TO THE ACCOMPLISHMENTS OF

MODERN ENGINEERING. AND

THROUGHOUT ITS COURSE, THE

ROAD RISES TO ITS PURPOSE

OF MOBILITY.

4.

INDEX

ART DIRECTORS/DESIGNERS

PHOTOGRAPHERS/ ILLUSTRATORS